Sentence Starters

Abdullahi Hagar

Copyright 2020 © by Abdullahi Hagar
All rights reserved

No part of this publication may be reproduced or distributed in print or electronic form without prior permission of the author.

Please respect the hard work of the author and do not participate in or encourage the piracy of copyrighted materials.

Other books by Abdullahi Hagar

Emotions Thesaurus
Sentence Thesaurus
Dialogue Tags
Transistional Words & Phrases
Adjective Thesaurus
Adverb Thesaurus
Verb Thesaurus

A

abandoned *verb*
I abandoned my...
I abandoned the...

abandonment *noun*
Abandonment lingered in...

absorbed *verb*
I absorbed my...
I absorbed the...

accelerated *verb*
I accelerated the...
I accelerated down the...
I accelerated onto a...
I accelerated out of the...

accepted *verb*
I accepted a\an\the...
I accepted my...

accessed *verb*
I accessed my...
I accessed the...

accompanied *verb*
I accompanied the...

accounted *verb*
I accounted for the...

ached *verb*
I ached at the...
I ached for my...
I ached for the...
I ached in a...
I ached with an\the...

achieved *verb*
I achieved a...
I achieved my...

acknowledged *verb*
I acknowledged my...
I acknowledged the...
I acknowledged with a...

acquired *verb*
I acquired the...
I acquired during my...
I acquired during the...

acted *verb*
I acted the...
I acted in the...
I acted like a\an\the...
I acted out a...
I acted with a...
I acted without a...

activated *verb*
I activated my...
I activated the...

added *verb*
I added a\an\the...
I added my...
I added in a\the...
I added in my...
I added on a\the...
I added to my...
I added to the...
I added under my...
I added up my...

I added with an...

addressed *verb*
I addressed an\the...
I addressed my...

adjusted *verb*
I adjusted a\an\the...
I adjusted my...
I adjusted on the...

administered *verb*
I administered a...

admiration *noun*
Admiration glinted in...
My admiration grew for...

admired *verb*
I admired my...
I admired the...

admitted *verb*
I admitted a\the...
I admitted my...
I admitted to my...
I admitted to the...

adopted *verb*
I adopted a\an\the...

adored *verb*
I adored my...
I adored the...

adrenaline *noun*
Adrenaline coursed through...
Adrenaline coursed throughout...
Adrenaline dumped into...
Adrenaline poured into...

Adrenaline poured through...
Adrenaline shot through...
Adrenaline spilled into...
Adrenaline surged in...
Adrenaline surged into...
Adrenaline surged through...
Adrenaline tripped into...
My adrenaline flowed as...

advanced *verb*
I advanced a\the...
I advanced my...
I advanced in an...
I advanced into the...
I advanced on my...
I advanced on the...
I advanced through the...
I advanced to the...
I advanced toward the...
I advanced until the...
I advanced upon the...
I advanced with my...

advertised *verb*
I advertised the...

advised *verb*
I advised the...
I advised against the...

affected *verb*
I affected a...

affixed *verb*
I affixed a...

afternoon *noun*
Afternoon drifted into...
Afternoon passed into...
Afternoon slid toward...

The afternoon drew down
around...

aggression *noun*
Aggression built in...

agitation *noun*
Agitation rolled from...

agony *noun*
Agony arced through...
Agony exploded behind...
Agony lanced through...
Agony lashed through...
Agony ripped through...
Agony splintered through...

agreed *verb*
I agreed on a\the...
I agreed to a\an\the...
I agreed with the...

aimed *verb*
I aimed a\the...
I aimed my...
I aimed along the...
I aimed at a\the...
I aimed for a\an\the...

air *noun*
The air billowed up in...
The air shuddered out of...
The air slammed out of...
The air sucked out of...
The air went out of...

aired *verb*
I aired the...

alarm *noun*

Alarm blazed across...
Alarm bled into...
Alarm clamored through...
Alarm flickered in...
Alarm shot through...
Alarm stirred inside...
Alarms sounded amid...
Alarms went off in...
An alarm rang in
My alarm deepened as...
An alarm went off in...
My alarm went off at...

alleged *verb*
I alleged in the...

alley *noun*
The alley came out on...

allowed *verb*
I allowed a\the...
I allowed my...

altered *verb*
I altered my...
I altered the...

alternated *verb*
I alternated my...
I alternated between the...
I alternated until the...

ambled *verb*
I ambled along the...
I ambled in the...
I ambled to the...
I ambled up the...
I ambled off into the...
I ambled over to the...

amended *verb*

I amended my...

amusement *noun*

Amusement flickered across...
Amusement flickered in...
Amusement flickered over...
Amusement glittered in...
Amusement shone in...
Amusement twinkled in...
Amusement warred with...

analyzed *verb*

I analyzed the...

anchored *verb*

I anchored my...
I anchored for the...
I anchored in a...

anger *noun*

Anger blazed through...
Anger blossomed on...
Anger boiled through...
Anger congealed in...
Anger coursed through...
Anger fizzed through...
Anger flared in...
Anger flared within...
Anger flashed across...
Anger flashed in...
Anger flashed on...
Anger flushed through...
Anger glinted in...
Anger knotted with...
Anger pricked at...
Anger ripped through...
Anger shot like...
Anger sizzled behind...
Anger sloshed through...
Anger smoldered behind...

Anger surged in...
Anger surged inside...
Anger surged over...
Anger surged through...
Anger washed through...
An anger rose in
Anger boiled up in...
Anger boiled up inside...
Anger welled up in...
My anger boiled at...
My anger came off...
My anger collapsed like...
My anger crashed over...
The anger went from
My anger boiled over at...
My anger went out of...
The anger leapt out of...
The anger roiled along like...

angled *verb*

I angled a\the...
I angled my...
I angled along an...
I angled for the...
I angled through the...
I angled toward the...

anguish *noun*

Anguish shone in...
Anguish tore at...
Anguish came out of...

animal *noun*

The animal went down with...

animosity *noun*

Animosity poured out of...

ankle *noun*

My ankle felt like...
My ankle screamed as...

announced *verb*

I announced an\the...
I announced my...
I announced to the...

annoyance *noun*

Annoyance flashed in...
Annoyance flashed over...
Annoyance sparked in...

answer *noun*

An answer appeared on
My answer came in...
My answer came without...
My answers came in...
The answer came from
The answer came in
The answer emerged from
The answer slipped out of...

answered *verb*

I answered a\an\the...
I answered my...
I answered after a\the...
I answered at the...
I answered in a\the...
I answered on the...
I answered over my...
I answered with a...
I answered with my...
I answered without a...

anticipated *verb*

I anticipated a...

anticipation *noun*

Anticipation coursed through...
Anticipation shot through...
Anticipation simmered as...

Anticipation thrummed
through...
Anticipation tugged at...
Anticipation washed through...

anxiety *noun*

Anxiety ate at...
Anxiety clutched at...
Anxiety crept into...
Anxiety gnawed at...
Anxiety shot through...
Anxiety spiked through...
Anxiety tingled in...
Anxiety uncoiled in...
Anxiety warred with...

apologized *verb*

I apologized because the...
I apologized for my...
I apologized for the...
I apologized to the...

appealed *verb*

I appealed to my...

appeared *verb*

I appeared a\the...
I appeared as a\an...
I appeared at my...
I appeared at the...
I appeared in an\the...
I appeared inside a...
I appeared on a...
I appeared out of the...

applause *noun*

Applause broke out among...
Applause broke out around...
Applause went up from...
My armpits felt like...

applied *verb*

I applied a\the...
I applied my...
I applied for a\an...
I applied to a\the...

appreciated *verb*

I appreciated a\the...
I appreciated at my...

apprehension *noun*

Apprehension washed over...

approached *verb*

I approached a\the...
I approached my...
I approached from the...
I approached with my...
I approached with the...

approved *verb*

I approved the...
I approved of my...
I approved of the...

arced *verb*

I arced my...
I arced across the...
I arced off the...

arched *verb*

I arched a\an\the...
I arched my...
I arched into a\the...
I arched off the...
I arched out of the...
I arched up to the...

argued *verb*

I argued the...
I argued for a\an...
I argued with my...
I argued with the...

arm *noun*

Arms hung through...
Arms wrapped around...
An arm went under
Arms extended out at...
My arm came around...
My arm dropped like...
My arm hung from...
My arm moved in...
My arm screamed in...
My arm shook as...
My arm tightened around...
My arm went about...
My arm went around...
My arms came about...
My arms came around...
My arms closed around...
My arms closed over...
My arms felt like...
My arms groped for...
My arms screamed with...
My arms shook as...
My arms slid around...
My arms slid under...
My arms slipped around...
My arms wavered as...
My arms went around...
My arms went in...
The arm felt like
My arm came down against...
My arm came up in...
My arm drove out in...
My arm flopped down by...
My arm shot out like...
My arm shot out of...
My arms came up around...
My arms lay out of...

My arms swept up in...

armed *verb*

I armed my...

aroma *noun*

The aroma wafted up from...

arousal *noun*

Arousal arced through...
Arousal hummed from...
Arousal sparked inside...
Arousal spiraled through...
Arousal stirred inside...
Arousal stirred like...
Arousal surged through...
Arousal roared up on...
My arousal came against...

arranged *verb*

I arranged a\the...
I arranged my...
I arranged for a\the...

arrested *verb*

I arrested a...
I arrested my...

arrived *verb*

I arrived a\the...
I arrived at a\an\the...
I arrived at my...
I arrived beneath the...
I arrived during the...
I arrived for my...
I arrived for the...
I arrived in my...
I arrived in the...
I arrived inside the...
I arrived like a...

I arrived on a\the...
I arrived outside the...
I arrived via a...
I arrived with a...
I arrived with my...
I arrived without the...

arrow *noun*

Arrows flew through...
Arrows hissed past...
Arrows shot at...
Arrows whizzed toward...
Arrows soared out from...
Arrows stuck out of...
The arrow streaked down from...

ascended *verb*

I ascended a\the...
I ascended at a...
I ascended by a...
I ascended from the...
I ascended into the...
I ascended to the...

ash *noun*

The ashes went out with...

asked *verb*

I asked a\the...
I asked my...
I asked about my...
I asked about the...
I asked after a...
I asked after my...
I asked around the...
I asked as a\the...
I asked at the...
I asked before my...
I asked for a\an\the...
I asked for my...
I asked if a\an\the...

I asked if my...
I asked in a\the...
I asked in my...
I asked into the...
I asked of the...
I asked over my...
I asked through the...
I asked under my...
I asked while the...
I asked with a\an...

assailed *verb*

I assailed the...

assaulted *verb*

I assaulted an...

assembled *verb*

I assembled a\the...
I assembled my...
I assembled after the...
I assembled by the...

assessed *verb*

I assessed my...
I assessed the...

assumed *verb*

I assumed a\the...
I assumed my...
I assumed from my...
I assumed from the...

assured *verb*

I assured the...

ate *verb*

I ate a\an\the...
I ate my...
I ate about a...

I ate after the...
I ate at a\the...
I ate despite the...
I ate for a...
I ate from a\the...
I ate in a\the...
I ate in my...
I ate like a...
I ate on a\the...
I ate on my...
I ate up the...
I ate with my...

attached *verb*

I attached a\the...
I attached my...

attack *noun*

The attack broke off as...

attacked *verb*

I attacked a\the...
I attacked my...

attempted *verb*

I attempted a\an\the...

attended *verb*

I attended a\the...
I attended to the...
I attended until the...

attention *noun*

My attention fell on...

authorized *verb*

I authorized the...

averted *verb*

I averted my...

avoided *verb*
I avoided the...

awaited *verb*
I awaited my...

awakened *verb*
I awakened a...
I awakened my...
I awakened from a...
I awakened to the...

awareness *noun*
Awareness dawned in...
Awareness faded from...
Awareness prickled along...
Awareness prickled over...
Awareness sizzled across...

awkwardness *noun*
Awkwardness morphed into...

awoke *verb*
I awoke a\an\the...
I awoke at the...
I awoke because a...
I awoke during the...
I awoke from a...
I awoke in a\the...
I awoke on the...
I awoke to a\the...
I awoke with a\an\the...

axe *noun*
My axe fell from...
My axe lay by...
An axe came down on...
The axe flew out of...

B

babbled *verb*

I babbled a...
I babbled like a...
I babbled out the...

back *noun*

My back broke as...

backed *verb*

I backed a\the...
I backed my...
I backed across the...
I backed against the...
I backed along the...
I backed around the...
I backed away a...
I backed down the...
I backed into a\an\the...
I backed off a\the...
I backed out the...
I backed through a...
I backed to the...
I backed toward my...
I backed toward the...
I backed until the...
I backed up a\the...
I backed down into a...
I backed off from the...
I backed off on a...
I backed out at the...
I backed out of my...
I backed out of the...
I backed out onto the...
I backed out with a...
I backed out without a...
I backed up against a\the...

I backed up to my...
I backed up to the...
I backed up toward the...
I backed up until my...

backhanded *verb*

I backhanded the...

backtracked *verb*

I backtracked in a...
I backtracked to the...

bade *verb*

I bade my...
I bade the...

badged *verb*

I badged my...
I badged the...

bag *noun*

A bag fell over in...
The bag fell out of...

bagged *verb*

I bagged a\the...

bailed *verb*

I bailed a...

baked *verb*

I baked a...
I baked in the...

balanced *verb*

I balanced a\the...
I balanced my...
I balanced at the...
I balanced for a...
I balanced on the...

balked *verb*

I balked at my...
I balked at the...

ball *noun*

The ball winked out of...

balled *verb*

I balled my...
I balled the...
I balled up my...
I balled up the...

bandaged *verb*

I bandaged the...

banged *verb*

I banged an\the...
I banged my...
I banged against a...
I banged on the...
I banged open a\the...
I banged over the...
I banged up my...
I banged around in the...
I banged out of the...

banished *verb*

I banished my...
I banished the...

banked *verb*

I banked the...
I banked below the...
I banked into the...
I banked through a...
I banked to the...

bar *noun*

The bar dropped down into...
The bar skidded out of...

bared *verb*

I bared my...

bargained *verb*

I bargained away my...

barged *verb*

I barged between the...
I barged into the...
I barged past the...

barked *verb*

I barked a\an...
I barked my...
I barked at my...
I barked into my...
I barked into the...
I barked out a\an...
I barked out my...

barred *verb*

I barred the...

barreled *verb*

I barreled down the...
I barreled into the...
I barreled through the...

bashed *verb*

I bashed my...
I bashed the...
I bashed at an...

bathed *verb*

I bathed my...
I bathed the...
I bathed in the...

batted *verb*

I batted my...
I batted the...
I batted at the...
I batted down the...

battered *verb*

I battered the...

battle *noun*

The battle loomed up out...

battled *verb*

I battled a...
I battled my...
I battled in the...
I battled through the...
I battled with the...

beamed *verb*

I beamed a...
I beamed my...
I beamed at my...
I beamed at the...
I beamed out at the...

beast *noun*

The beast wanted out so...

beat *verb*

I beat a\the...
I beat my...
I beat against the...
I beat at the...
I beat on the...
I beat up my...
I beat up the...

became *verb*

I became a\an\the...
I became like a\an...
I became like my...

beckoned *verb*

I beckoned a\the...
I beckoned my...
I beckoned for the...
I beckoned to a\an\the...
I beckoned with my...

bed *noun*

The bed looked out of...
The bed moved out from...

bedded *verb*

I bedded a\the...
I bedded down the...

beeped *verb*

I beeped my...

beer *noun*

The beer came along with...

began *verb*

I began a\an\the...
I began my...
I began as a...
I began at the...
I began in a\the...
I began with a\an\the...

begged *verb*

I begged my...
I begged the...
I begged for a\an\the...
I begged on the...
I begged with my...

behaved *verb*

I behaved like a...
I behaved on the...

beheld *verb*

I beheld a...

believed *verb*

I believed my...
I believed the...
I believed from the...
I believed if the...
I believed in a\the...
I believed in my...
I believed on my...

bell *noun*

My bells rang with...

bellow *noun*

A bellow shot out of...

bellowed *verb*

I bellowed a...
I bellowed my...
I bellowed at my...
I bellowed at the...
I bellowed from my...
I bellowed like a...
I bellowed past the...
I bellowed to the...

belonged *verb*

I belonged at the...
I belonged in an\the...
I belonged to my...
I belonged to the...
I belonged with my...

belted *verb*

I belted my...
I belted on my...

bent *verb*

I bent a\the...
I bent my...
I bent across the...
I bent at the...
I bent down the...
I bent for a...
I bent in the...
I bent into the...
I bent like a...
I bent open the...
I bent over a\the...
I bent over my...
I bent to my...
I bent to the...
I bent toward the...
I bent down at the...
I bent down from my...
I bent down over the...
I bent over at the...

berated *verb*

I berated the...

bet *verb*

I bet a\an\the...
I bet my...
I bet on the...

betrayed *verb*

I betrayed my...
I betrayed the...

bewilderment *noun*

Bewilderment flickered in...
Bewilderment stirred in...

biceps *noun*
My biceps looked like...

bid *verb*
I bid my...

bile *noun*
Bile burned in...
Bile churned in...
Bile climbed into...
Bile rose at...
Bile rose from...
Bile rose in...
Bile rose into...
Bile seeped into...
My bile rose at...

bird *noun*
Birds broke from...
Birds cried from...
Birds flew across...
Birds flew over...
Birds returned from...
Birds sang above...
Birds sang in...
A bird flew up from...
The bird hopped up onto...
The bird peered down at...
The bird tumbled down in...

bit *verb*
I bit my...
I bit the...
I bit at my...
I bit at the...
I bit into a\the...
I bit into my...
I bit off a\the...
I bit on my...
I bit out a...
I bit down against my...

I bit down on my...
I bit down on the...

bitched *verb*
I bitched a...

bitterness *noun*
Bitterness flooded through...
Bitterness welled up within...
My bitterness felt like...

blacked *verb*
I blacked out for a...
I blacked out from the...
I blacked out in the...

blackness *noun*
Blackness bloomed in...
Blackness crept in...
Blackness poured from...
Blackness pressed at...
Blackness tumbled toward...
The blackness spilled out of...

blade *noun*
Blades flashed in...
Blades hung like...
My blade came with...
My blade slammed into...
The blade plunged into
The blade sang as
The blade sank in
The blade sank into
The blade slid from
A blade scythed out of...
My blade plunged down through...
My blade swung across at...
The blade cut down like...
The blade flew out of...
The blade struck out like...
The blade tore down through...

blamed *verb*
I blamed my...
I blamed the...

blanched *verb*
I blanched at the...

blanked *verb*
I blanked out the...
I blanked out for a...

blasted *verb*
I blasted a\the...
I blasted my...

blazed *verb*
I blazed through the...

bled *verb*
I bled a...
I bled for the...
I bled into the...
I bled like a...

blended *verb*
I blended into the...

blessed *verb*
I blessed the...

blew *verb*
I blew a\an\the...
I blew my...
I blew across the...
I blew in a...
I blew off the...
I blew on a\the...
I blew on my...
I blew out a\an\the...
I blew out my...
I blew over the...
I blew past the...
I blew through my...
I blew through the...
I blew with a...

blinked *verb*
I blinked a\an\the...
I blinked my...
I blinked against my...
I blinked against the...
I blinked as a\the...
I blinked as my...
I blinked at my...
I blinked at the...
I blinked away a\the...
I blinked away my...
I blinked for a...
I blinked in the...
I blinked into the...
I blinked open my...
I blinked past the...
I blinked through my...
I blinked through the...
I blinked up at the...

blocked *verb*
I blocked a\the...
I blocked out my...
I blocked out the...

blood *noun*
Blood bloomed from...
Blood bloomed like...
Blood blossomed at...
Blood blossomed in...
Blood bubbled over...
Blood bubbled through...
Blood dribbled from...
Blood dripped between...

Blood dripped from...
Blood dripped in...
Blood dripped into...
Blood dripped onto...
Blood erupted from...
Blood exploded from...
Blood fell in...
Blood flew from...
Blood flew in...
Blood flew into...
Blood flowed from...
Blood flowed in...
Blood flowed into...
Blood flowed through...
Blood frothed at...
Blood geysered from...
Blood gleamed at...
Blood glistened from...
Blood gouted from...
Blood gurgled into...
Blood gushed against...
Blood gushed from...
Blood gushed in...
Blood gushed into...
Blood gushed on...
Blood gushed over...
Blood haloed around...
Blood jetted onto...
Blood leaked from...
Blood misted into...
Blood mushroomed from...
Blood oozed between...
Blood oozed from...
Blood oozed onto...
Blood oozed through...
Blood poured between...
Blood poured from...
Blood poured onto...
Blood poured over...
Blood poured through...
Blood puddled around...
Blood pumped from...

Blood ran from...
Blood ran in...
Blood ran into...
Blood ran on...
Blood roared in...
Blood roared through...
Blood rose from...
Blood rushed from...
Blood rushed in...
Blood rushed into...
Blood rushed onto...
Blood rushed through...
Blood sang in...
Blood seeped from...
Blood seeped through...
Blood shot from...
Blood showed on...
Blood sizzled on...
Blood smeared in...
Blood soaked through...
Blood spattered from...
Blood spattered on...
Blood spewed from...
Blood spilled from...
Blood spilled onto...
Blood spilled over...
Blood splashed onto...
Blood splattered into...
Blood splattered like...
Blood splattered on...
Blood spluttered through...
Blood spouted from...
Blood sprayed across...
Blood sprayed as...
Blood sprayed from...
Blood sprayed into...
Blood sprayed on...
Blood sprayed through...
Blood spurted from...
Blood started from...
Blood streamed from...
Blood surged from...

Blood surged into...
Blood surged like...
Blood surged through...
Blood trailed from...
Blood trickled from...
Blood trickled through...
Blood welled around...
Blood welled between...
Blood welled from...
Blood bubbled out of...
Blood bubbled up from...
Blood bubbled up in...
Blood burst out in...
Blood came out in...
Blood cried down like...
Blood dribbled out of...
Blood flew up from...
Blood flowed out of...
Blood gushed out as...
Blood gushed out from...
Blood gushed out of...
Blood pattered down on...
Blood popped out on...
Blood poured out in...
Blood seeped down from...
Blood seeped out around...
Blood seeped out between...
Blood seeped out of...
Blood shot out of...
Blood spat out from...
Blood sprayed out across...
Blood sprayed out of...
Blood spurted out as...
Blood streamed out of...
Blood surged out of...
Blood threaded down from...
Blood trickled down across...
Blood welled out between...
Blood welled up at...
Blood welled up from...
My blood boiled at...
My blood felt like...

My blood raced through...
My blood rushed in...
My blood rushed through...
My blood sang in...
My blood screamed in...
My blood seeped into...
My blood surged into...
My blood surged with...
The blood ran across
The blood rushed from
The blood rushed through
The blood fell out of...
The blood gushed out in...
The blood rushed out of...

bloodied *verb*
I bloodied my...

blossomed *verb*
I blossomed into a...

blotted *verb*
I blotted my...

blow *noun*
Blows exploded against...
Blows rained down on...
My blows landed like...
The blows landed on

blundered *verb*
I blundered through the...

blurted *verb*
I blurted the...
I blurted out a\the...

blushed *verb*
I blushed a...
I blushed at the...

I blushed in the...
I blushed like a...
I blushed to my...

boarded *verb*

I boarded a\an\the...
I boarded in a...

boasted *verb*

I boasted a...

boat *noun*

The boat moved out upon...
The boat passed out at...
The boat slipped out of...

bobbed *verb*

I bobbed a...
I bobbed my...
I bobbed in the...

body *noun*

Bodies closed in...
Bodies erupted in...
Bodies floated in...
Bodies surged through...
Bodies tumbled in...
A body landed on
A body lay by
A body permeated with
A\the body lay on...
Bodies piled up in...
Bodies pressed up against...
Bodies shambled out of...
My body arched into...
My body arched over...
My body boiled with...
My body bowed with...
My body crashed into...
My body crashed through...
My body drooped between...

My body dropped like...
My body erupted into...
My body exploded into...
My body fell in...
My body felt as...
My body felt like...
My body felt on...
My body landed on...
My body lay against...
My body lay in...
My body moved against...
My body moved before...
My body moved beyond...
My body opened for...
My body plummeted from...
My body plunged below...
My body quaked as...
My body quaked with...
My body recovered from...
My body reflected in...
My body responded with...
My body sagged against...
My body sagged over...
My body screamed at...
My body screamed for...
My body shook as...
My body shook in...
My body shook with...
My body shrieked in...
My body slammed against...
My body slammed into...
My body slid under...
My body stirred on...
My body surged under...
My body tensed under...
My body tightened into...
My body worked like...
My body wove into...
The body crashed into
The body exploded in
The body thrashed for
My body arched up for...

My body came down over...
My body came up against...
My body gave out at...
My body leapt out of...
My body went down in...
The body slid out from...

boggled *verb*

I boggled at the...

boiled *verb*

I boiled the...

bolted *verb*

I bolted a\the...
I bolted across the...
I bolted down a\an...
I bolted for the...
I bolted from my...
I bolted from the...
I bolted into the...
I bolted out the...
I bolted past the...
I bolted through the...
I bolted to a...
I bolted to my...
I bolted toward the...
I bolted up the...
I bolted off into the...
I bolted out into the...
I bolted out of my...
I bolted out of the...
I bolted up to the...

bomb *noun*

A bomb went off at...

bonded *verb*

I bonded over the...
I bonded with the...

bone *noun*

Bone crackled as...
Bone crunched under...
Bone grated on...
Bones crunched between...
Bones popped as...
Bones snapped with...
Bones pressed out against...

book *noun*

Books fell around...
Books made out of...

booked *verb*

I booked a...
I booked my...

boom *noun*

A boom rang out in...
The boom telescoped up toward...

boomed *verb*

I boomed at the...

boosted *verb*

I boosted my...
I boosted the...

boot *noun*

A\the boot slammed into...
My boot hung over...
My boots felt like...
My boots rang against...
My boot came down on...
The boot came down on...

booted *verb*

I booted a...
I booted up my...
I booted up the...

bore *verb*

I bore a\the...
I bore my...
I bore for a...

boredom *noun*

My boredom felt like...

borrowed *verb*

I borrowed a\the...
I borrowed against my...

bottom *noun*

The bottom dropped out of...
The bottom fell out of...

bought *verb*

I bought a\an\the...
I bought my...
I bought at a\the...
I bought for my...
I bought for the...
I bought from an\the...
I bought from my...
I bought in the...
I bought with my...

bounced *verb*

I bounced a\the...
I bounced my...
I bounced across the...
I bounced along the...
I bounced from the...
I bounced in my...
I bounced off an\the...
I bounced on my...
I bounced onto my...
I bounced to my...
I bounced along in the...
I bounced up over the...

bound *verb*

I bound an\the...
I bound my...
I bound around the...
I bound down the...
I bound up the...

bounded *verb*

I bounded across the...
I bounded down the...
I bounded from the...
I bounded over the...
I bounded through the...
I bounded to my...
I bounded to the...
I bounded up the...
I bounded up from my...
I bounded up from the...
I bounded up off the...

bow *noun*

The bow rose up in...

bowed *verb*

I bowed my...
I bowed at the...
I bowed from the...
I bowed in a...
I bowed off the...
I bowed to my...
I bowed to the...
I bowed with a...
I bowed with my...
I bowed out of the...

bowl *noun*

The bowl slipped out of...

boxed *verb*
I boxed up my...

braced *verb*
I braced a\the...
I braced my...
I braced for an\the...
I braced up my...

bragged *verb*
I bragged about my...

brain *noun*
My brain felt like...
My brain ran through...
My brain scrambled for...
My brain went into...

braked *verb*
I braked the...
I braked at a\the...
I braked for the...
I braked in the...
I braked to a...

branch *noun*
Branches hung over...
Branches rubbed against...
Branches slapped at...
Branches snapped on...
Branches tore at...

brandished *verb*
I brandished a\the...
I brandished my...

braved *verb*
I braved the...

breached *verb*
I breached the...

breakfast *noun*
Breakfast sat on...

breast *noun*
My breasts bounced as...
My breasts shook with...

breath *noun*
Breath gusted from...
Breath hissed from...
Breath hissed through...
Breath steamed on...
Breaths went by...
Breath exploded out of...
Breath hissed out from...
Breath shot out of...
My breath blew over...
My breath came in...
My breath came through...
My breath drew in...
My breath escaped in...
My breath escaped on...
My breath exhaled in...
My breath froze as...
My breath raced between...
My breath rushed between...
My breath smelled like...
My breath smelled near...
My breath smelled of...
My breath stank like...
My breath stank of...
My breath stirred against...
My breath tore at...
My breath went in...
My breaths came in...
The breath hissed from
A breath came out of...
My breath came out in...
My breath heaved out of...

My breath hiccupped out of...
My breath hissed out at...
My breath hissed out between...
My breath hissed out in...
My breath leaked out of...
My breath oofed out of...
My breath plumed out on...
My breath raced out of...
My breath rasped out of...
My breath rushed out of...
My breath sawed out of...
My breath shot out of...
My breath sped up as...
My breath tore out of...
My breath went out of...
My breath whooshed out of...
The breath knocked out of...
The breath rasped out of...
The breath smoked out of...
The breath went out of...
The breath whooshed out of...

breathed *verb*

I breathed a\an\the...
I breathed for a...
I breathed for my...
I breathed in a\the...
I breathed into the...
I breathed like a...
I breathed on the...
I breathed out a\the...
I breathed out my...
I breathed through my...
I breathed through the...

breathing *noun*

My breathing slowed as...
My breathing sounded like...
My breathing sped up until...

breeze *noun*

A breeze kicked up as...
A breeze wafted up from...

breezed *verb*

I breezed along the...
I breezed past the...
I breezed through the...

brewed *verb*

I brewed a...

bribed *verb*

I bribed the...

briefed *verb*

I briefed the...

brightened *verb*

I brightened a...
I brightened my...
I brightened at the...
I brightened into a...
I brightened like the...
I brightened up a...

bristled *verb*

I bristled a...
I bristled at the...

broached *verb*

I broached the...

broke *verb*

I broke a\the...
I broke my...
I broke about an...
I broke at the...
I broke before the...
I broke down the...
I broke for the...

I broke from the...
I broke inside the...
I broke into a\an\the...
I broke like a...
I broke off a\the...
I broke off my...
I broke open a\the...
I broke through a\the...
I broke to the...
I broke up a...
I broke off as a\the...
I broke off as my...
I broke off for a...
I broke off in a...
I broke off on a...
I broke off with a...
I broke out in a...
I broke out into the...
I broke out of my...
I broke out of the...
I broke out onto the...
I broke out with a...
I broke through to the...

brooded *verb*

I brooded the...
I brooded for a...

brought *verb*

I brought a\an\the...
I brought my...
I brought about the...
I brought along the...
I brought down a\the...
I brought in a\the...
I brought out a\the...
I brought out my...
I brought over a...
I brought up a\the...
I brought up my...
I brought down upon my...

I brought out of the...
I brought up from the...

brow *noun*

My brow dropped in...
My brows dropped into...
My brows rose at...
My brows rose in...
My brows rose with...
My brow drew down as...
My brow drew down in...
My brow drew down into...
My brows cranked down on...
My brows rose up like...
My brows went up in...

browsed *verb*

I browsed a\the...
I browsed for a...
I browsed through the...

brushed *verb*

I brushed a\an\the...
I brushed my...
I brushed aside my...
I brushed aside the...
I brushed at a\the...
I brushed at my...
I brushed away a\the...
I brushed off a\the...
I brushed off my...
I brushed out my...
I brushed out the...
I brushed past the...
I brushed up a...
I brushed up on the...

bucked *verb*

I bucked my...
I bucked against my...
I bucked on the...

buckled *verb*

I buckled a...
I buckled my...
I buckled on my...
I buckled on the...
I buckled over the...

bugged *verb*

I bugged the...

building *noun*

Buildings disappeared behind...
Buildings flashed by...

built *verb*

I built a\an\the...
I built my...
I built for the...
I built into the...
I built up my...
I built up the...
I built with my...

bulged *verb*

I bulged my...

bullet *noun*

Bullet wound in...
Bullets dug through...
Bullets exploded from...
Bullets rained through...
Bullets sizzled past...
Bullets slammed into...
Bullets tore into...
Bullets zipped past...
A bullet exploded in
A bullet glanced against
A bullet went through
A\the bullet slammed into...

Bullets rang out from...
My bullet blasted into...
My bullet went through...
The bullet blew through
The bullet exploded through

bullied *verb*

I bullied the...

bumped *verb*

I bumped my...
I bumped against the...
I bumped into a\the...
I bumped into my...
I bumped open the...

bunched *verb*

I bunched my...
I bunched the...
I bunched toward the...
I bunched up my...
I bunched up the...

bundled *verb*

I bundled my...
I bundled up my...

buried *verb*

I buried a\the...
I buried my...

burned *verb*

I burned a\the...
I burned my...
I burned down a...
I burned during the...
I burned for a...
I burned in a...
I burned like the...
I burned on the...

I burned through the...
I burned with an...

burnt *verb*

I burnt my...
I burnt the...

burrowed *verb*

I burrowed a...
I burrowed my...
I burrowed into the...

burst *verb*

I burst out into a...
I burst out of the...
I burst out onto the...

bus *noun*

A bus pulled up at...
The bus lumbered along like...
The buses moved off from...

busied *verb*

I busied my...

bust *verb*

I bust my...

busted *verb*

I busted the...
I busted out a...
I busted up a...
I busted out of the...
I busted up with my...

bustled *verb*

I bustled around behind the...
I bustled off without a...

butted *verb*

I butted my...
I butted out my...

buttock *noun*

My buttocks came out of...
My buttocks swelled out into...

buttoned *verb*

I buttoned my...
I buttoned up my...
I buttoned up the...

buzzed *verb*

I buzzed my...
I buzzed at the...
I buzzed down my...
I buzzed down the...

bypassed *verb*

I bypassed my...
I bypassed the...

C

cab *noun*
The cab pulled over in...
The cab sped along as...

cackled *verb*
I cackled my...
I cackled at my...
I cackled at the...
I cackled like a...

calculated *verb*
I calculated the...
I calculated in my...

call *noun*
Calls came from...

called *verb*
I called a\an\the...
I called my...
I called about an\the...
I called around the...
I called because the...
I called down the...
I called for a\an\the...
I called for my...
I called from a\the...
I called in a\the...
I called in my...
I called into my...
I called into the...
I called on my...
I called on the...
I called out a\the...
I called over a...
I called over my...
I called through the...
I called to my...
I called to the...
I called up a\an\the...
I called up my...
I called upon my...
I called upon the...
I called across to the...
I called out across the...
I called out in a\the...
I called out into the...
I called out over my...
I called out through the...
I called out to a\the...
I called out to my...
I called out with a...
I called over to the...
I called up to the...

calm *noun*
Calm drifted through...
Calm landed on...
Calm moved with...
Calm settled over...
Calm stood over...
Calm dropped down over...

calmed *verb*
I calmed my...
I calmed down a...

came *verb*
I came a\the...
I came about a...
I came across a\an\the...
I came after my...
I came around a\the...
I came around my...
I came around the...
I came at a\the...

I came by my...
I came by the...
I came down the...
I came for a\an\the...
I came for my...
I came from a\the...
I came in a\the...
I came in my...
I came into a\an\the...
I came into my...
I came like an...
I came near the...
I came of my...
I came off the...
I came on a\the...
I came onto the...
I came out a\the...
I came over a\the...
I came past the...
I came through a\the...
I came through my...
I came to a\an\the...
I came to my...
I came toward the...
I came under a...
I came up the...
I came upon a\an\the...
I came upon my...
I came with a\an\the...
I came with my...
I came within a...
I came across as a...
I came along for the...
I came around into the...
I came around on the...
I came around to the...
I came around with my...
I came down for an...
I came down from the...
I came down off my...
I came down off the...
I came down on a\the...

I came down on my...
I came down onto the...
I came off as a\the...
I came out at a...
I came out behind the...
I came out for a\the...
I came out in a\an...
I came out into a\the...
I came out of a\the...
I came out of my...
I came out on the...
I came out through the...
I came out to the...
I came out with the...
I came over as an...
I came over from the...
I came over on my...
I came over to the...
I came through to the...
I came through with the...
I came up along the...
I came up as the...
I came up behind the...
I came up beside the...
I came up for a...
I came up from my...
I came up from the...
I came up inside the...
I came up off the...
I came up on a\the...
I came up on my...
I came up onto my...
I came up to my...
I came up to the...
I came up with a\the...

camera *noun*

Cameras clicked as...
Cameras mounted in...
The camera focused down on...
The camera zoomed out as...

camped *verb*

I camped beside the...
I camped by a...
I camped in a\the...
I camped on an...
I camped under the...
I camped out with a...

canceled *verb*

I canceled my...
I canceled the...

cancelled *verb*

I cancelled my...

candle *noun*

Candles flickered in...
Candles flickered on...
Candles hung in...
The candle leaped up with...

candlelight *noun*

Candlelight flickered against...
Candlelight flickered in...
Candlelight shimmered over...

cantered *verb*

I cantered my...
I cantered along the...
I cantered up the...

capped *verb*

I capped my...
I capped the...

captured *verb*

I captured a\the...

car *noun*

Cars crunched across...
Cars emerged on...
Cars lumbered by...
Cars moved past...
Cars moved through...
Cars sped by...
Cars stopped at...
Cars whizzed past...
A car appeared at
A car appeared from
A car came around
A car drew alongside
A car flashed by
A car rumbled past
A car rushed by
A car stopped on
A car went by
The car continued by
The car continued on
The car disappeared from
The car drove by
The car jumped into
The car leaped across
The car moved toward
The car opened on
The car raced on
The car sat at
The car screamed at
The car screamed into
The car shook as
The car skidded on
The car slid into
The car slowed as
The car slowed on
The car smelled like
The car smelled of
The car sputtered at
The car stayed in
The car stood at
The car waited for
The car went into
The car went through

The car yanked in
A car drew up beside...
A car pulled up as...
A car swept out of...
My car pulled up behind...
My car started up in...
The car hummed along at...
The car launched up onto...
The car pulled out into...
The car pulled up in...
The car roared up over...
The car sped along under...
The car sped out of...
The car took off at...

cared *verb*

I cared about my...
I cared about the...
I cared for the...

careened *verb*

I careened around the...
I careened through the...

caress *noun*

My caress felt like...

caressed *verb*

I caressed the...

carriage *noun*

The carriage came out into...

carried *verb*

I carried a\an\the...
I carried my...
I carried in my...
I carried on a\the...
I carried out my...
I carried within my...

I carried around like a...

carted *verb*

I carted off the...

carved *verb*

I carved a\the...
I carved into my...
I carved through the...

cashed *verb*

I cashed my...
I cashed the...
I cashed in my...
I cashed in the...
I cashed out for a...

cast *verb*

I cast a\an\the...
I cast my...
I cast about the...
I cast aside the...
I cast down my...
I cast into the...
I cast off my...
I cast out my...
I cast up my...
I cast around in my...
I cast around in the...

cat *noun*

The cat blinked up at...
The cat held out for...
The cat jumped up beside...
The cat looked up at...
The cat moved over at...
The cat padded along beside...
The cat rubbed up against...
The cats came out of...
The cats sat down in...

caught *verb*

I caught a\an\the...
I caught my...
I caught at a\the...
I caught at my...
I caught up a...
I caught on to the...
I caught up at the...
I caught up in a\an...
I caught up on the...
I caught up to my...
I caught up to the...
I caught up with my...
I caught up with the...

caused *verb*

I caused a\the...

caution *noun*

Caution disappeared in...
Caution flickered over...
Caution fought with...

cawed *verb*

I cawed my...

ceased *verb*

I ceased my...

celebrated *verb*

I celebrated my...
I celebrated into the...

cellar *noun*

The cellar opened up before...

centered *verb*

I centered my...
I centered the...

certainty *noun*

Certainty settled in...
My certainty dwindled with...

chafed *verb*

I chafed a...
I chafed at the...

chair *noun*

Chairs moved behind...
My chair overturned at...
The chair came with
The chair flew across
The chair slammed against
My chair tipped over with...
The chair tipped over for...

chanced *verb*

I chanced a...

changed *verb*

I changed a\an\the...
I changed my...
I changed for the...
I changed from a\the...
I changed in a...
I changed into a...
I changed into my...
I changed out my...
I changed to a\an...
I changed out of my...

channeled *verb*

I channeled my...

chant *noun*

Chants rose for...

chanted *verb*

I chanted a...

I chanted with the...

chaos *noun*

Chaos foamed in...
Chaos reigned as...
Chaos reigned in...
Chaos roared in...
Chaos ruled in...

charge *noun*

The charge blew out of...

charged *verb*

I charged the...
I charged across the...
I charged along the...
I charged down the...
I charged for the...
I charged in a...
I charged into the...
I charged through the...
I charged to my...
I charged toward the...
I charged towards the...
I charged up the...
I charged with the...
I charged out of the...

chased *verb*

I chased my...
I chased the...
I chased away the...
I chased down the...

chasm *noun*

A chasm opened up in...

chatted *verb*

I chatted about the...
I chatted for a\an...

I chatted on the...
I chatted with a\the...

cheated *verb*

I cheated a\the...
I cheated my...
I cheated at the...
I cheated with a...

checked *verb*

I checked an\the...
I checked my...
I checked around the...
I checked at a\the...
I checked behind the...
I checked for a\an...
I checked in a...
I checked inside the...
I checked into a\the...
I checked into my...
I checked on my...
I checked on the...
I checked out my...
I checked out the...
I checked over my...
I checked over the...
I checked through the...
I checked under the...
I checked with a\the...
I checked down between the...
I checked in to a\the...
I checked out after the...
I checked out from the...
I checked out of the...

cheek *noun*

My cheek fell into...
My cheek lay over...
My cheek rested against...
My cheeks felt like...
My cheeks yanked up in...

cheer *noun*

A cheer went up as...
A cheer went up at...
A cheer went up from...
A cheer went up into...
A cheer went up on...

cheered *verb*

I cheered as a...
I cheered at the...

cherished *verb*

I cherished the...

chest *noun*

My chest caved in...
My chest felt like...
My chest moved against...
My chest rumbled beneath...
My chest sank in...
My chest shook as...
My chest tightened at...
My chest tightened with...
My chest eased down over...
My chest seized up in...

chewed *verb*

I chewed a\the...
I chewed my...
I chewed at my...
I chewed at the...
I chewed for a...
I chewed like a...
I chewed on a\the...
I chewed on my...

chill *noun*

Chills shot through...
Chills swept through...
Chills went over...
A chill crawled over
A chill descended over
A chill raced across
A chill ran through
A chill shuttered through
A chill stole over
A chill went through
My chill came from...

chime *noun*

Chimes went off in...

chin *noun*

My chin dropped at...
My chin rested on...
My chin rubbed along...
My chin went up in...

chipped *verb*

I chipped off the...

chirped *verb*

I chirped my...

choice *noun*

A choice made out of...

choked *verb*

I choked a\the...
I choked down my...
I choked for a...
I choked in a...
I choked off a...
I choked off my...
I choked on a\the...
I choked on my...
I choked out a\the...

chopped *verb*

I chopped the...
I chopped down with my...

chopper *noun*
The chopper touched down on...

chose *verb*
I chose a\an\the...
I chose my...
I chose as my...
I chose of my...

chucked *verb*
I chucked the...
I chucked up the...

chuckle *noun*
A chuckle rumbled out of...

chuckled *verb*
I chuckled a...
I chuckled as the...
I chuckled at my...
I chuckled at the...
I chuckled under my...

chugged *verb*
I chugged the...
I chugged around a...

churned *verb*
I churned the...

cigarette *noun*
A cigarette appeared between
A cigarette hung from
My cigarette paused in...
The cigarette dropped from

cinched *verb*

I cinched my...
I cinched the...

circled *verb*
I circled a\the...
I circled my...
I circled about a...
I circled around the...
I circled as the...
I circled behind the...
I circled for a...
I circled through the...
I circled to the...
I circled around to the...

cited *verb*
I cited the...

city *noun*
A city sprouted up in...
The city hunkered down on...
The city rose up against...
The city rose up behind...
The city spread out before...

claimed *verb*
I claimed a\the...

clambered *verb*
I clambered my...
I clambered down the...
I clambered into the...
I clambered off the...
I clambered on the...
I clambered onto my...
I clambered onto the...
I clambered over a\the...
I clambered through the...
I clambered to my...
I clambered up a\the...
I clambered down into the...

I clambered on to a...
I clambered up into the...
I clambered up on the...
I clambered up onto the...

clamped *verb*

I clamped a\the...
I clamped my...
I clamped down on my...
I clamped down on the...

clanged *verb*

I clanged the...

clanked *verb*

I clanked the...

clapped *verb*

I clapped a\the...
I clapped my...
I clapped as the...
I clapped at the...
I clapped on my...
I clapped with the...

clasped *verb*

I clasped a\the...
I clasped my...

class *noun*

The class froze along with...

clattered *verb*

I clattered across the...
I clattered down the...
I clattered onto the...
I clattered through the...
I clattered up the...
I clattered out of the...

claw *noun*

Claws dug in...
Claws rasped as...
Claws ripped at...
Claws sank into...
Claws scored across...
My claws dug into...
My claws sank into...

clawed *verb*

I clawed my...
I clawed the...
I clawed at my...
I clawed at the...
I clawed for my...
I clawed for the...

cleaned *verb*

I cleaned my...
I cleaned the...
I cleaned away the...
I cleaned like a...
I cleaned off the...
I cleaned out a\the...
I cleaned out my...
I cleaned up a\the...
I cleaned up my...
I cleaned up around the...
I cleaned up in the...

cleared *verb*

I cleared a\the...
I cleared my...
I cleared away an\the...
I cleared off a...
I cleared off my...

clenched *verb*

I clenched my...
I clenched the...

clicked *verb*

I clicked a\the...
I clicked my...
I clicked down a...
I clicked off a\the...
I clicked off my...
I clicked on my...
I clicked on the...
I clicked open a\the...
I clicked out of my...

climax *noun*

My climax came on...

climaxed *verb*

I climaxed in a...
I climaxed with a...

climbed *verb*

I climbed a\the...
I climbed my...
I climbed above the...
I climbed astride the...
I climbed behind the...
I climbed between the...
I climbed down a\the...
I climbed from the...
I climbed in the...
I climbed inside the...
I climbed into a\the...
I climbed into my...
I climbed like a...
I climbed off my...
I climbed off the...
I climbed on the...
I climbed onto a\the...
I climbed onto my...
I climbed out a\the...
I climbed over a\the...
I climbed past the...
I climbed through a\the...

I climbed to a\the...
I climbed to my...
I climbed toward the...
I climbed towards the...
I climbed under the...
I climbed underneath the...
I climbed up the...
I climbed down for the...
I climbed down from my...
I climbed down from the...
I climbed down into the...
I climbed down off the...
I climbed out into the...
I climbed out of my...
I climbed out of the...
I climbed out with the...
I climbed out without a...
I climbed up behind the...
I climbed up into the...
I climbed up near the...
I climbed up on the...
I climbed up onto the...
I climbed up through a...
I climbed up to the...

clinked *verb*

I clinked my...
I clinked the...

clipped *verb*

I clipped my...
I clipped the...
I clipped on a...
I clipped up a...

clit *noun*

My clit felt like...

cloak *noun*

Cloak died in...
My cloak hung from...

My cloak lay over...
My cloak streamed behind...

closed *verb*

I closed a\the...
I closed my...
I closed about the...
I closed down my...
I closed down the...
I closed out a...
I closed with the...

clothing *noun*

The clothing morphed along with...

cloud *noun*

Clouds floated around...
Clouds hung across...
Clouds massed in...
Clouds raced across...
Clouds slid across...
Clouds rolled out of...

clouded *verb*

I clouded a...

clucked *verb*

I clucked a...
I clucked my...

clumped *verb*

I clumped down the...
I clumped through the...

clung *verb*

I clung by my...
I clung for a...
I clung to my...
I clung to the...

I clung on to my...
I clung on to the...

clunked *verb*

I clunked my...

clustered *verb*

I clustered around the...

clutched *verb*

I clutched a\the...
I clutched my...
I clutched at a\the...
I clutched at my...
I clutched for my...
I clutched in my...

coasted *verb*

I coasted until my...

coated *verb*

I coated a...

coaxed *verb*

I coaxed the...

cobweb *noun*

Cobwebs brushed at...

cock *noun*

My cock felt like...
My cock jumped in...
My cock lay between...
My cock leaped within...
My cock looked as...
My cock plunged into...
My cock responded with...
My cock screamed for...
My cock stirred at...
My cock swelled in...

My cock tightened behind...
My cock hung down between...

cocked *verb*

I cocked a\an\the...
I cocked my...

coffee *noun*

Coffee sloshed from...
Coffee spilled across...
Coffee splashed on...
Coffee tasted like...

coin *noun*

Coins clicked on...
Coins clinked as...
Coins rained onto...

collapsed *verb*

I collapsed a\the...
I collapsed across the...
I collapsed against a\the...
I collapsed amid the...
I collapsed at the...
I collapsed from the...
I collapsed in a\the...
I collapsed into a\the...
I collapsed into my...
I collapsed like a\an...
I collapsed on my...
I collapsed on the...
I collapsed onto my...
I collapsed onto the...
I collapsed over the...
I collapsed to my...
I collapsed to the...

collar *noun*

My collar dug into...

collected *verb*

I collected a\the...
I collected my...
I collected along the...
I collected up my...
I collected up the...

collided *verb*

I collided into the...
I collided with a\an\the...

color *noun*

Color bled from...
Color bloomed in...
Color came into...
Color rose in...
Colors broke through...
Colors deepened as...
Colors shrieked at...
Colors jumped out like...
Colors swirled up against...

colored *verb*

I colored a...
I colored my...

column *noun*

The column broke down in...

combed *verb*

I combed my...
I combed the...
I combed at my...
I combed through my...
I combed through the...

command *noun*

The command came out of...
The command rushed out of...

commanded *verb*
I commanded a\the...
I commanded my...

commented *verb*
I commented on the...

committed *verb*
I committed a\the...

communicated *verb*
I communicated through the...

compared *verb*
I compared a\the...

compassion *noun*
Compassion reflected in...

complained *verb*
I complained about a...
I complained about my...

completed *verb*
I completed an\the...
I completed my...

composed *verb*
I composed a\the...
I composed my...
I composed for the...

comprehension *noun*
Comprehension came over...
Comprehension dawned on...
Comprehension filtered into...

concealed *verb*
I concealed a...

I concealed my...

conceded *verb*
I conceded a\the...
I conceded with a...

conceived *verb*
I conceived a...

concentrated *verb*
I concentrated a...
I concentrated for a...
I concentrated on my...
I concentrated on the...

concentration *noun*
Concentration increased by...

concern *noun*
Concern emanated from...
Concern flickered in...
Concern ran like...
Concern spiked through...

concluded *verb*
I concluded my...
I concluded the...
I concluded with a\the...

concocted *verb*
I concocted a...

concurred *verb*
I concurred with the...

conducted *verb*
I conducted a...
I conducted my...

conferred *verb*

I conferred with the...

confessed *verb*

I confessed my...
I confessed the...
I confessed in a...
I confessed of my...
I confessed to my...

confided *verb*

I confided my...
I confided during the...

confirmed *verb*

I confirmed the...
I confirmed with a\the...

confiscated *verb*

I confiscated from the...

confronted *verb*

I confronted my...
I confronted the...

confusion *noun*

Confusion bled into...
Confusion erupted within...
Confusion flashed through...
Confusion flickered across...
Confusion flickered in...
Confusion jabbed through...
Confusion reigned amongst...
Confusion roared through...
Confusion roiled within...
Confusion swept over...
Confusion swept through...
Confusion swirled inside...
Confusion tumbled through...
My confusion exploded into...

conjured *verb*

I conjured the...
I conjured up an...

connected *verb*

I connected my...
I connected the...
I connected on my...
I connected to the...
I connected with a\the...

conquered *verb*

I conquered my...

conscience *noun*

My conscience stirred inside...

consciousness *noun*

Consciousness returned in...

considered *verb*

I considered a\the...
I considered my...
I considered for a...

consisted *verb*

I consisted of a...

conspired *verb*

I conspired with a...

constituted *verb*

I constituted a...

consulted *verb*

I consulted a\the...
I consulted my...
I consulted in my...
I consulted with a...

contacted *verb*
I contacted an\the...
I contacted my...

contemplated *verb*
I contemplated my...
I contemplated the...

contempt *noun*
Contempt boiled up in...
Contempt boiled up inside...

contentment *noun*
Contentment slid through...

continued *verb*
I continued a\the...
I continued my...
I continued along the...
I continued around the...
I continued at a...
I continued down the...
I continued for a...
I continued in a\the...
I continued in my...
I continued into the...
I continued on my...
I continued over the...
I continued past an\the...
I continued through the...
I continued to the...
I continued toward the...
I continued up the...
I continued with my...
I continued with the...
I continued on to my...
I continued on to the...
I continued out of the...

contorted *verb*
I contorted my...

contributed *verb*
I contributed to the...

control *noun*
My control slipped for...

controlled *verb*
I controlled my...
I controlled the...

converged *verb*
I converged toward the...

conversation *noun*
Conversation resumed among...
Conversation resumed in...
Conversation wandered through...
Conversations ceased in...
Conversations halted in...
The conversation kept up in...

converted *verb*
I converted the...
I converted to a...

conveyed *verb*
I conveyed the...

conviction *noun*
Conviction coursed through...

convulsed *verb*
I convulsed as the...
I convulsed on a...
I convulsed under the...

cooked *verb*
I cooked a\the...

I cooked for the...

cooled *verb*
I cooled my...

cop *noun*
A cop crouched down beside...
A cop sent up for...
The cop crawled up into...
The cop reached down for...

copied *verb*
I copied my...
I copied the...
I copied down the...

core *noun*
My core grabbed onto...
My core tightened at...
My core tightened in...

corner *noun*
A corner flaked off between...

corresponded *verb*
I corresponded for a...

coughed *verb*
I coughed a...
I coughed after a...
I coughed as the...
I coughed at the...
I coughed in the...
I coughed into a\the...
I coughed into my...
I coughed on a...
I coughed out a...
I coughed out my...
I coughed up a\the...

counseled *verb*
I counseled my...

counted *verb*
I counted a\the...
I counted my...
I counted down the...
I counted in my...
I counted off my...
I counted off the...
I counted on the...
I counted out the...
I counted up the...
I counted down in my...

countered *verb*
I countered with a...
I countered with my...

courage *noun*
Courage surged through...

covered *verb*
I covered a\the...
I covered my...

coveted *verb*
I coveted as a...

cowered *verb*
I cowered against the...
I cowered at my...
I cowered in my...

crack *noun*
Cracks appeared along...
Cracks appeared in...
Cracks erupted across...
Cracks raced through...
Cracks spiraled around...

A crack ran down through...

cracked *verb*

I cracked a\an\the...
I cracked my...
I cracked open a\an\the...
I cracked up a...

cradled *verb*

I cradled a\the...
I cradled my...

crafted *verb*

I crafted a...

crammed *verb*

I crammed a\the...
I crammed my...

craned *verb*

I craned my...

cranked *verb*

I cranked my...
I cranked the...
I cranked down my...
I cranked on the...
I cranked open the...
I cranked up the...

crashed *verb*

I crashed a\the...
I crashed my...
I crashed across the...
I crashed against the...
I crashed down the...
I crashed in a...
I crashed into a\the...
I crashed on a\the...
I crashed through a\the...

I crashed to the...
I crashed down onto the...
I crashed down with a...
I crashed out of the...

craved *verb*

I craved a\an\the...
I craved like a...

crawled *verb*

I crawled across the...
I crawled along the...
I crawled between the...
I crawled down the...
I crawled from the...
I crawled in my...
I crawled in the...
I crawled inside the...
I crawled into a\the...
I crawled into my...
I crawled onto the...
I crawled out my...
I crawled over the...
I crawled through the...
I crawled to my...
I crawled to the...
I crawled toward the...
I crawled under my...
I crawled under the...
I crawled up the...
I crawled out of my...
I crawled out of the...
I crawled out through a...
I crawled over to the...

created *verb*

I created a\the...
I created my...
I created in the...
I created with my...
I created without the...

creature *noun*

The creature came out of...
The creature dropped down on...
The creature glared up at...
The creature went down on...

crept *verb*

I crept a...
I crept across the...
I crept along the...
I crept around the...
I crept behind a\the...
I crept down the...
I crept from my...
I crept from the...
I crept in a\the...
I crept into a\the...
I crept into my...
I crept off an...
I crept through the...
I crept to a\the...
I crept to my...
I crept toward the...
I crept up the...
I crept off into the...
I crept out into the...
I crept over to the...
I crept up to the...

cried *verb*

I cried a\the...
I cried my...
I cried as an...
I cried at the...
I cried because the...
I cried for a\the...
I cried for my...
I cried in a...
I cried into the...
I cried like a...

I cried out my...
I cried to the...
I cried until my...
I cried with the...
I cried out against a...
I cried out as a\the...
I cried out as my...
I cried out at the...
I cried out for a...
I cried out in my...
I cried out in the...
I cried out to the...
I cried out with the...

cringed *verb*

I cringed a...
I cringed as the...
I cringed at the...
I cringed into the...

crinkled *verb*

I crinkled my...

crisscrossed *verb*

I crisscrossed the...

croak *noun*

A croak came out of...

croaked *verb*

I croaked the...
I croaked out a...
I croaked with a...

crooked *verb*

I crooked a\the...
I crooked my...

crossed *verb*

I crossed a\the...

I crossed my...
I crossed above the...
I crossed in a...
I crossed into the...
I crossed out the...
I crossed over the...
I crossed through a\the...
I crossed to a\the...
I crossed to my...
I crossed toward the...
I crossed with the...
I crossed out of the...
I crossed over to the...

crouched *verb*

I crouched against the...
I crouched at a\the...
I crouched behind a\the...
I crouched behind my...
I crouched below the...
I crouched beside the...
I crouched by the...
I crouched in a\the...
I crouched in my...
I crouched on my...
I crouched on the...
I crouched over the...
I crouched so my...
I crouched under a\the...
I crouched with my...
I crouched down at the...
I crouched down in the...
I crouched down on my...

crowded *verb*

I crowded around the...
I crowded at the...
I crowded into the...
I crowded near a...
I crowded on the...

crowed *verb*

I crowed my...

cruised *verb*

I cruised along a...
I cruised down the...
I cruised through the...
I cruised up my...
I cruised up the...

crumbled *verb*

I crumbled the...
I crumbled to the...

crumpled *verb*

I crumpled the...
I crumpled against my...
I crumpled at the...
I crumpled into a...
I crumpled on the...
I crumpled to my...
I crumpled to the...
I crumpled up the...
I crumpled with a...
I crumpled without a...

crunched *verb*

I crunched the...
I crunched on a\an...
I crunched up the...
I crunched down on my...

crushed *verb*

I crushed my...
I crushed the...
I crushed out my...

cry *noun*

Cries rose from...
A cry slipped past

A cry tore from
Cries went up from...
My cry started as...
The cry came from
The cry died in
The cry tore at
A cry rang out from...
A cry went up from...
My cry boiled out of...

cued *verb*

I cued up the...

cuffed *verb*

I cuffed the...

cup *noun*

The cup slipped out of...

cupped *verb*

I cupped a\the...
I cupped my...

curiosity *noun*

Curiosity boiled inside...
Curiosity demanded that...
Curiosity simmered in...
Curiosity snuck through...

curled *verb*

I curled a\an\the...
I curled my...
I curled around my...
I curled in the...
I curled into a\the...
I curled on my...
I curled over my...
I curled up against the...
I curled up in a\the...
I curled up in my...

I curled up on my...
I curled up on the...
I curled up under the...

curse *noun*

A curse blasted out of...
A curse leaked out of...
The curse exploded out of...

cursed *verb*

I cursed my...
I cursed the...
I cursed against the...
I cursed as my...
I cursed through my...
I cursed under my...
I cursed with an...

curved *verb*

I curved my...

cut *verb*

I cut a\an\the...
I cut my...
I cut across the...
I cut around the...
I cut at a...
I cut away a\the...
I cut between the...
I cut down the...
I cut for the...
I cut into my...
I cut into the...
I cut off a\the...
I cut off my...
I cut open a...
I cut out the...
I cut through a\the...
I cut to my...
I cut to the...
I cut up a...

I cut across with my...
I cut down with my...
I cut off as the...
I cut off with a...
I cut up from an...

D

dabbed *verb*

I dabbed a\the...
I dabbed my...
I dabbed at a\the...
I dabbed at my...
I dabbed away the...
I dabbed on my...

damned *verb*

I damned the...
I damned up the...

danced *verb*

I danced a\the...
I danced my...
I danced among the...
I danced around a...
I danced around the...
I danced as the...
I danced beneath the...
I danced for an\the...
I danced into the...
I danced like a...
I danced on a...
I danced under the...
I danced until my...
I danced until the...
I danced within the...
I danced around like a...
I danced out from the...

danger *noun*

Danger gleamed in...
Danger lurked in...

dangled *verb*

I dangled the...
I dangled over the...

dared *verb*

I dared a...

darkened *verb*

I darkened my...
I darkened with a...

darkness *noun*

Darkness came in...
Darkness closed around...
Darkness crashed in...
Darkness crowded in...
Darkness descended with...
Darkness dwelled in...
Darkness fell around...
Darkness fell like...
Darkness fell on...
Darkness fell outside...
Darkness fell over...
Darkness fell upon...
Darkness flickered at...
Darkness flickered in...
Darkness flooded in...
Darkness gathered around...
Darkness gathered at...
Darkness gathered beyond...
Darkness hung over...
Darkness lashed at...
Darkness lay beyond...
Darkness settled in...
Darkness settled over...
Darkness spilled from...
Darkness sucked at...
Darkness surged against...
Darkness swam before...
Darkness tumbled through...
Darkness came up at...

Darkness foamed up on...
Darkness rippled out from...

darted *verb*

I darted a...
I darted my...
I darted across the...
I darted after the...
I darted along the...
I darted behind a...
I darted down the...
I darted from my...
I darted from the...
I darted in the...
I darted into the...
I darted past the...
I darted through a\the...
I darted to my...
I darted to the...
I darted toward the...
I darted off down the...
I darted out of the...
I darted over to my...
I darted over to the...

dashed *verb*

I dashed across the...
I dashed against the...
I dashed around the...
I dashed away the...
I dashed down the...
I dashed from my...
I dashed from the...
I dashed in the...
I dashed into the...
I dashed off my...
I dashed out the...
I dashed past the...
I dashed through the...
I dashed to the...
I dashed up the...

I dashed off down the...
I dashed out of the...
I dashed out to my...

dated *verb*

I dated a\the...
I dated for a...

dawn *noun*

Dawn arrived in...
Dawn arrived with...
Dawn broke as...
Dawn broke like...
Dawn came in...
Dawn lived in...
Dawn stole into...

daylight *noun*

Daylight came in...
Daylight flooded into...
Daylight flooded through...
Daylight mingled with...
Daylight poured in...
Daylight spilled through...
Daylight streamed in...
Daylight streamed through...
Daylight shone down through...

deactivated *verb*

I deactivated the...

dealt *verb*

I dealt a\the...
I dealt out the...
I dealt with a\the...
I dealt with my...

death *noun*

Death came in...
Death followed in...

Death grunted with...
Death hung in...
Death hung like...
Death pivoted toward...
Death raced towards...
Death reached for...
Death brushed up against...
Death spun out of...
My death did in...

debated *verb*

I debated my...
I debated the...
I debated for a...

debris *noun*

Debris fell as...
Debris flew into...
Debris lay in...
Debris rained for...

decided *verb*

I decided a\an\the...
I decided my...
I decided after a...
I decided at the...
I decided in the...
I decided on a\an\the...
I decided within a...

deck *noun*

A deck jutted out toward...

declared *verb*

I declared my...
I declared the...

declined *verb*

I declined the...

decorated *verb*

I decorated the...

decreased *verb*

I decreased my...
I decreased the...

decreed *verb*

I decreed the...

deepened *verb*

I deepened my...
I deepened the...

defeated *verb*

I defeated a\the...

defended *verb*

I defended the...

defense *noun*

Defense increased by...

defiance *noun*

Defiance churned in...

defied *verb*

I defied the...

deflated *verb*

I deflated a...
I deflated into my...
I deflated into the...
I deflated like a...

deflected *verb*

I deflected a\the...

delayed *verb*

I delayed the...

deleted *verb*
I deleted my...
I deleted the...

delight *noun*
Delight bloomed on...

delighted *verb*
I delighted in the...

delivered *verb*
I delivered a\an\the...
I delivered my...

delved *verb*
I delved into a\the...

demanded *verb*
I demanded a\the...
I demanded my...
I demanded of the...

dematerialized *verb*
I dematerialized under the...

demonstrated *verb*
I demonstrated my...

denial *noun*
Denial boiled in...

denied *verb*
I denied the...

dented *verb*
I dented my...
I dented the...

departed *verb*
I departed the...
I departed for the...
I departed from the...

depended *verb*
I depended on the...

deployed *verb*
I deployed my...
I deployed the...
I deployed with the...

deposited *verb*
I deposited an\the...
I deposited my...

depressed *verb*
I depressed my...
I depressed the...

descended *verb*
I descended the...
I descended at a...
I descended from the...
I descended into a\the...
I descended to the...
I descended upon the...
I descended out of the...

described *verb*
I described a\the...
I described my...

deserted *verb*
I deserted my...

deserved *verb*
I deserved a\an\the...

I deserved my...

designed *verb*
I designed the...

desire *noun*
Desire burned in...
Desire coiled within...
Desire coursed through...
Desire hummed between...
Desire ignited in...
Desire rolled off...
Desire rose around...
Desire shot through...
Desire simmered in...

desired *verb*
I desired a...

despair *noun*
Despair drifted through...
Despair moved through...
Despair raced through...
Despair swept over...
Despair tugged at...
Despair washed over...
Despair washed through...

despaired *verb*
I despaired as the...

desperation *noun*
Desperation broke into...
Desperation clutched at...
Desperation welled inside...

despised *verb*
I despised my...
I despised the...

destroyed *verb*
I destroyed a\the...
I destroyed my...
I destroyed to my...

destruction *noun*
Destruction called for...

detached *verb*
I detached my...
I detached the...
I detached with a...

detail *noun*
The details came up in...

detailed *verb*
I detailed a\the...
I detailed my...

detected *verb*
I detected a\an\the...

determination *noun*
Determination rolled off...
My determination bled into...

determined *verb*
I determined the...

detested *verb*
I detested the...

devastated *verb*
I devastated the...

developed *verb*
I developed a\an...
I developed in the...

devoted *verb*

I devoted an\the...
I devoted my...

devotion *noun*

Devotion smoldered in...

devoured *verb*

I devoured my...
I devoured the...

dialed *verb*

I dialed a\an\the...
I dialed my...
I dialed in the...
I dialed up my...
I dialed up the...

dialled *verb*

I dialled the...

dick *noun*

My dick agreed because...

dictated *verb*

I dictated my...

did *verb*

I did a\an\the...
I did my...
I did about the...
I did after a...
I did as a\the...
I did at the...
I did before my...
I did during my...
I did during the...
I did for a\the...
I did from a...

I did in my...
I did in the...
I did like a\the...
I did on the...
I did open the...
I did to my...
I did until my...
I did up my...
I did up the...
I did with a\an\the...
I did with my...

died *verb*

I died a...
I died aboard my...
I died about a...
I died because the...
I died before my...
I died by the...
I died during a\the...
I died for a...
I died from an\the...
I died in a\the...
I died in my...
I died of a\an...
I died on a\the...
I died on my...
I died upon the...
I died with a\the...
I died with my...
I died without a...

differed *verb*

I differed from the...

dimmed *verb*

I dimmed the...

dimple *noun*

My dimples deepened along
with...

dined *verb*

I dined on an...

dipped *verb*

I dipped a\the...
I dipped my...
I dipped into a\the...
I dipped under a\the...
I dipped down for a...
I dipped off into the...

directed *verb*

I directed my...
I directed the...

dirt *noun*

Dirt dug into...
Dirt spilled into...
Dirt blew up beside...
Dirt flew up at...

disabled *verb*

I disabled the...

disagreed *verb*

I disagreed about the...

disappeared *verb*

I disappeared a\the...
I disappeared around a\the...
I disappeared at a...
I disappeared behind the...
I disappeared beneath an\the...
I disappeared down the...
I disappeared for a\the...
I disappeared from my...
I disappeared from the...
I disappeared in a\the...
I disappeared inside the...
I disappeared into a\an\the...
I disappeared into my...
I disappeared on my...
I disappeared through a\the...
I disappeared with my...

disappointment *noun*

Disappointment emanated from...
Disappointment flared over...
Disappointment flooded
through...
Disappointment nagged at...
Disappointment pierced
through...
Disappointment settled over...
Disappointment surged over...
Disappointment throbbed in...
Disappointment washed
through...
My disappointment felt like...

disapproved *verb*

I disapproved of the...

disbelief *noun*

Disbelief collided with...
Disbelief raged through...
Disbelief registered on...
Disbelief roared through...

discarded *verb*

I discarded the...

discomfort *noun*

Discomfort crawled across...

disconnected *verb*

I disconnected the...
I disconnected as the...

discovered *verb*
I discovered a\an\the...
I discovered from an...

discussed *verb*
I discussed a\the...

disembarked *verb*
I disembarked at the...
I disembarked outside the...

disengaged *verb*
I disengaged my...
I disengaged the...
I disengaged with my...

disentangled *verb*
I disentangled my...

dish *noun*
The dishes piled up on...

disintegrated *verb*
I disintegrated in a...

disliked *verb*
I disliked the...

dislodged *verb*
I dislodged a...

dismay *noun*
Dismay clutched at...
Dismay grappled with...
Dismay swept through...

dismissed *verb*
I dismissed my...
I dismissed the...

dismounted *verb*
I dismounted a\the...
I dismounted at the...
I dismounted beside a...
I dismounted by the...
I dismounted for a...
I dismounted in a...

dispatched *verb*
I dispatched a...

dispersed *verb*
I dispersed a...

displayed *verb*
I displayed a\the...
I displayed my...

displeasure *noun*
Displeasure registered on...

disregarded *verb*
I disregarded the...

dissolved *verb*
I dissolved into the...

distress *noun*
Distress radiated from...
My distress grew as...

ditched *verb*
I ditched my...
I ditched the...

dived *verb*
I dived across the...
I dived for a\the...
I dived into the...

I dived through an...
I dived to the...
I dived under the...
I dived with the...

diverted *verb*

I diverted my...
I diverted the...
I diverted to the...

divided *verb*

I divided my...
I divided the...

divorced *verb*

I divorced a...
I divorced my...

dizziness *noun*

Dizziness broke over...
Dizziness slammed into...
Dizziness swooped through...
Dizziness washed over...

docked *verb*

I docked the...
I docked at a...

doctored *verb*

I doctored my...

dodged *verb*

I dodged a\the...
I dodged around a...
I dodged around the...
I dodged behind a...
I dodged into the...
I dodged over the...
I dodged through a...
I dodged out of the...

dog *noun*

Dogs barked as...
Dogs moved between...
The dog glanced up at...
The dog looked up at...
The dog roared off in...
The dog stood up in...
The dog trotted along with...

doled *verb*

I doled out the...

dominated *verb*

I dominated the...

donated *verb*

I donated the...

donned *verb*

I donned a\the...
I donned my...

door *noun*

Doors opened on...
Doors slammed as...
The door rumbled up on...
The doors popped out of...

doorbell *noun*

My doorbell rang at...
The doorbell rang at

dotted *verb*

I dotted the...
I dotted at the...

double-checked *verb*

I double-checked my...
I double-checked the...

I double-checked with my...

doubled *verb*

I doubled my...
I doubled over the...
I doubled over in the...
I doubled over with a\the...

doubt *noun*

Doubt came into...
Doubt flickered through...
Doubt gnawed at...
Doubt mirrored in...
Doubt wormed into...
Doubts rushed at...
Doubt crept up on...
My doubt grew like...

doubted *verb*

I doubted a\the...
I doubted my...
I doubted if the...

doused *verb*

I doused my...
I doused the...

dove *verb*

I dove across the...
I dove around a...
I dove at the...
I dove beneath the...
I dove down an...
I dove for my...
I dove for the...
I dove in my...
I dove into a\the...
I dove off the...
I dove over the...
I dove through the...
I dove to the...

I dove toward the...
I dove under the...
I dove underneath a...

downed *verb*

I downed a\the...
I downed my...

downloaded *verb*

I downloaded an\the...
I downloaded my...

dozed *verb*

I dozed a...
I dozed as the...
I dozed for a...
I dozed in the...
I dozed off a...
I dozed on the...
I dozed off for a...
I dozed off with a...

drafted *verb*

I drafted a...

dragged *verb*

I dragged a\the...
I dragged my...
I dragged at my...
I dragged at the...
I dragged down the...
I dragged in a...
I dragged off my...
I dragged on a...
I dragged on my...
I dragged out a\the...
I dragged out my...
I dragged over a...
I dragged up a...

drained *verb*
I drained a\the...
I drained my...
I drained off the...

drank *verb*
I drank a\an\the...
I drank my...
I drank down a\the...
I drank for a...
I drank from a\the...
I drank from my...
I drank in the...
I drank like a...
I drank off my...
I drank off the...
I drank to my...
I drank until a\the...
I drank with my...
I drank out of my...

draped *verb*
I draped a\an\the...
I draped my...

drawled *verb*
I drawled the...

dread *noun*
Dread clawed at...
Dread closed in...
Dread coiled in...
Dread coiled inside...
Dread coiled within...
Dread fell on...
Dread gathered in...
Dread knotted in...
Dread mounted in...
Dread settled in...
Dread slammed into...
Dread squirmed in...

Dread swelled inside...
Dread swept over...
Dread trickled along...
Dread washed over...

dreaded *verb*
I dreaded the...

dreamed *verb*
I dreamed a\the...
I dreamed my...
I dreamed about my...
I dreamed about the...
I dreamed in the...
I dreamed of a\the...

dreamt *verb*
I dreamt a\an...
I dreamt my...
I dreamt of a\the...

drenched *verb*
I drenched the...

dress *noun*
The dress swirled out around...

dressed *verb*
I dressed the...
I dressed for a...
I dressed in a\the...
I dressed in my...
I dressed like a...
I dressed up as a...
I dressed up in my...

drew *verb*
I drew a\an\the...
I drew my...
I drew away my...

I drew down the...
I drew for my...
I drew for the...
I drew from a...
I drew in a\an...
I drew in my...
I drew on a\the...
I drew on my...
I drew open my...
I drew out a\an\the...
I drew out my...
I drew to a...
I drew to my...
I drew up a\an\the...
I drew up my...
I drew upon my...
I drew upon the...
I drew near to the...
I drew up against the...
I drew up at a...
I drew up onto my...

dried *verb*
I dried my...
I dried the...
I dried off my...

drifted *verb*
I drifted a...
I drifted my...
I drifted across the...
I drifted along the...
I drifted down the...
I drifted for a...
I drifted into a\an\the...
I drifted past the...
I drifted through a\the...
I drifted to my...
I drifted to the...
I drifted toward the...
I drifted up the...

I drifted off into an...
I drifted out into the...
I drifted out on the...
I drifted over to my...
I drifted over to the...
I drifted over toward the...

drilled *verb*
I drilled a...
I drilled as a...

dripped *verb*
I dripped my...
I dripped on the...

drizzle *noun*
The drizzle continued on until...

drone *noun*
The drone swooped down from...
The drone went out of...

drop *noun*
A drop rolled down over...

droplet *noun*
A droplet slid down from...

dropped *verb*
I dropped a\the...
I dropped my...
I dropped behind the...
I dropped below the...
I dropped by the...
I dropped down an\the...
I dropped during the...
I dropped from a\the...
I dropped in a...
I dropped in my...
I dropped into a\the...

I dropped into my...
I dropped like a...
I dropped off my...
I dropped off the...
I dropped on my...
I dropped onto the...
I dropped through the...
I dropped to a\the...
I dropped to my...
I dropped toward the...
I dropped within the...
I dropped down from the...
I dropped down in my...
I dropped down off my...
I dropped down off the...
I dropped down on my...
I dropped down on the...
I dropped down onto my...
I dropped down onto the...
I dropped down through the...
I dropped down with a...
I dropped on to the...
I dropped out of the...

drove *verb*

I drove a\an\the...
I drove my...
I drove about a\an...
I drove across the...
I drove alongside the...
I drove around the...
I drove at a...
I drove by a\the...
I drove down my...
I drove down the...
I drove for a\an...
I drove from the...
I drove in a\the...
I drove in my...
I drove into a\the...
I drove like a\an...

I drove near the...
I drove off the...
I drove on a\the...
I drove onto the...
I drove over a\the...
I drove past a\the...
I drove past my...
I drove through a\the...
I drove to a\the...
I drove to my...
I drove toward my...
I drove toward the...
I drove under a...
I drove until my...
I drove up the...
I drove with my...
I drove with the...
I drove around for a\an...
I drove around in a...
I drove around to the...
I drove down with the...
I drove off in my...
I drove out of the...
I drove out to the...
I drove over to the...
I drove up behind the...
I drove up on the...
I drove up to the...

drowned *verb*

I drowned in a\the...
I drowned in my...
I drowned on a...

drummed *verb*

I drummed a...
I drummed my...

ducked *verb*

I ducked a\the...
I ducked my...

I ducked around the...
I ducked as a\the...
I ducked at the...
I ducked behind a\an\the...
I ducked behind my...
I ducked beneath a\the...
I ducked beside the...
I ducked in the...
I ducked inside a\the...
I ducked into a\the...
I ducked into my...
I ducked out the...
I ducked past an...
I ducked through the...
I ducked to the...
I ducked under a\an\the...
I ducked underneath the...
I ducked down beneath the...
I ducked down in the...
I ducked out from the...
I ducked out of a...

dug *verb*

I dug a\the...
I dug my...
I dug at my...
I dug at the...
I dug for my...
I dug in my...
I dug in the...
I dug inside my...
I dug into my...
I dug into the...
I dug like a...
I dug out a\the...
I dug out my...
I dug through the...
I dug up a\the...
I dug with my...
I dug around in my...
I dug around in the...

I dug down in my...

dumped *verb*

I dumped a\the...
I dumped my...
I dumped out my...

dunked *verb*

I dunked a\the...
I dunked my...

dusk *noun*

Dusk lay over...
Dusk settled down about...

dust *noun*

Dust billowed from...
Dust billowed into...
Dust billowed through...
Dust blew in...
Dust churned in...
Dust dribbled from...
Dust fell from...
Dust flew from...
Dust geysered from...
Dust got in...
Dust hung in...
Dust lay over...
Dust lay upon...
Dust roiled over...
Dust rolled over...
Dust rose from...
Dust rose in...
Dust rose into...
Dust rose with...
Dust stirred from...
Dust swirled amid...
Dust swirled in...
Dust curled up in...
Dust flew up as...
Dust puffed out around...

Dust puffed up from...
Dust shot out of...
Dust went up in...

dusted *verb*

I dusted my...
I dusted the...
I dusted off my...

dwarfed *verb*

I dwarfed the...

dwelt *verb*

I dwelt by a\the...
I dwelt in the...
I dwelt on the...
I dwelt while my...

E

ear *noun*

My ear smelled of...
My ears felt like...
My ears rang with...

earned *verb*

I earned a\an\the...
I earned my...
I earned on the...

eased *verb*

I eased a\the...
I eased my...
I eased along the...
I eased down the...
I eased from my...
I eased from the...
I eased into a\the...
I eased into my...
I eased off the...
I eased onto the...
I eased open the...
I eased out the...
I eased through the...
I eased to the...
I eased toward the...
I eased around to the...
I eased down from the...
I eased down into a...
I eased down on the...
I eased down onto the...
I eased off into a...
I eased out into a...
I eased out of the...
I eased up on the...

echoed *verb*

I echoed the...

edged *verb*

I edged a\the...
I edged my...
I edged across the...
I edged alongside the...
I edged around the...
I edged behind the...
I edged into an\the...
I edged past the...
I edged through the...
I edged to the...
I edged toward the...
I edged out from the...
I edged out of the...
I edged over to the...
I edged up on my...
I edged up to the...

edited *verb*

I edited an...

ejected *verb*

I ejected the...

elation *noun*

Elation shot through...
Elation swept through...
My elation fell from...

elbow *noun*

My elbow rested on...

elbowed *verb*

I elbowed my...
I elbowed the...

electricity *noun*

Electricity arced between...
Electricity crackled in...
Electricity crackled over...
Electricity played over...
Electricity raced through...
Electricity sizzled through...
Electricity snapped through...
The electricity went out of...

elevated *verb*

I elevated my...

eliminated *verb*

I eliminated a...

emailed *verb*

I emailed a...
I emailed my...

e-mailed *verb*

I e-mailed a\the...

embarrassed *verb*

I embarrassed the...

embarrassment *noun*

Embarrassment flickered over...

embedded *verb*

I embedded a...
I embedded into the...

ember *noun*

Embers drifted through...

embraced *verb*

I embraced the...
I embraced for a...
I embraced in the...

emerged *verb*

I emerged a\an\the...
I emerged at the...
I emerged atop the...
I emerged behind the...
I emerged beneath a...
I emerged from a\an\the...
I emerged from my...
I emerged in a\the...
I emerged into a\an\the...
I emerged near the...
I emerged on the...
I emerged onto a\the...
I emerged through a...
I emerged with a...
I emerged out of the...

emitted *verb*

I emitted a...

emotion *noun*

Emotion erupted inside...
Emotion flickered across...
Emotion gathered in...
Emotion rippled over...
Emotion shimmered in...
Emotion stormed in...
Emotions flashed across...
Emotions flickered over...
Emotions played across...
Emotion growled out in...
Emotions welled up from...
My emotion seeped into...
My emotion swelled in...

emphasized *verb*

I emphasized the...
I emphasized at the...

employed *verb*

I employed a...

I employed my...

emptied *verb*

I emptied my...
I emptied the...
I emptied out my...

enchanted *verb*

I enchanted the...

encircled *verb*

I encircled the...

encountered *verb*

I encountered a\the...
I encountered in the...

encouraged *verb*

I encouraged the...

ended *verb*

I ended my...
I ended the...
I ended in a\the...
I ended on my...
I ended up a...
I ended with a...
I ended up as the...
I ended up at the...
I ended up in a\the...
I ended up on a\the...
I ended up with a\an\the...

endured *verb*

I endured a\the...

energy *noun*

The energy rushed out of...

engaged *verb*

I engaged my...
I engaged the...
I engaged in a\the...

engine *noun*

My engine sounded like...
The engine started on
The engine started with
The engine started up at...
The engine turned over with...

enhanced *verb*

I enhanced my...
I enhanced the...

enjoyed *verb*

I enjoyed a\the...
I enjoyed my...
I enjoyed about my...
I enjoyed in the...

enlarged *verb*

I enlarged my...
I enlarged the...

enlisted *verb*

I enlisted the...
I enlisted in the...

enrolled *verb*

I enrolled in the...

entered *verb*

I entered a\an\the...
I entered my...
I entered as a...
I entered in a...
I entered into a\the...
I entered through a\the...
I entered with a\the...

entertained *verb*
I entertained the...

enthusiasm *noun*
My enthusiasm trailed off with...

entrusted *verb*
I entrusted the...

envelope *noun*
An envelope slipped out of...

envied *verb*
I envied the...

envisioned *verb*
I envisioned a\an\the...
I envisioned my...

equipped *verb*
I equipped my...

erased *verb*
I erased the...

erupted *verb*
I erupted from my...
I erupted from the...
I erupted into the...

escaped *verb*
I escaped the...
I escaped by the...
I escaped for a...
I escaped from the...
I escaped into a\the...
I escaped out the...
I escaped with my...
I escaped with the...

escorted *verb*
I escorted the...

established *verb*
I established a...
I established my...

estimated *verb*
I estimated a\the...

etched *verb*
I etched in the...

evaded *verb*
I evaded the...

examined *verb*
I examined a\the...
I examined my...

exceeded *verb*
I exceeded my...

exchanged *verb*
I exchanged a\an...
I exchanged my...

excitement *noun*
Excitement coursed through...
Excitement curled in...
Excitement rose in...
Excitement rushed through...
Excitement shone on...
Excitement simmered in...
Excitement sizzled through...
Excitement surged in...
Excitement surged through...
Excitement tingled through...
My excitement lasted for...

My excitement mounted along
with...

exclaimed *verb*

I exclaimed with a...

excluded *verb*

I excluded the...

excused *verb*

I excused the...

executed *verb*

I executed a\the...

exerted *verb*

I exerted the...

exhaled *verb*

I exhaled a\an\the...
I exhaled my...
I exhaled as the...
I exhaled at the...
I exhaled in a...
I exhaled into the...
I exhaled on the...
I exhaled through my...

exhaustion *noun*

Exhaustion bled from...
Exhaustion dragged at...
Exhaustion flooded through...
Exhaustion lurked in...
My exhaustion felt like...

exhilaration *noun*

Exhilaration hurtled through...

existed *verb*

I existed as a...

I existed in a...
I existed on an...

exited *verb*

I exited the...
I exited at a...
I exited from a...
I exited into a\the...
I exited on my...
I exited on the...
I exited through the...
I exited to the...
I exited out to the...

expanded *verb*

I expanded my...
I expanded the...
I expanded into an...
I expanded on the...

expectation *noun*

Expectation coursed through...

expected *verb*

I expected a\an\the...
I expected my...

expelled *verb*

I expelled a...
I expelled my...

experience *noun*

Experience gained from...
Experience increased by...

experienced *verb*

I experienced a\an\the...
I experienced my...

explained *verb*

I explained my...
I explained the...
I explained about the...
I explained in the...
I explained on the...
I explained to my...
I explained to the...

exploded *verb*

I exploded my...
I exploded across the...
I exploded from the...
I exploded in a...
I exploded into the...
I exploded out the...
I exploded out of my...

explored *verb*

I explored the...

exposed *verb*

I exposed the...

expressed *verb*

I expressed my...

expression *noun*

My expression eased because...
My expression fell into...
My expression slipped from...
My expression tightened as...
My expression went from...

extended *verb*

I extended a\the...
I extended my...

extinguished *verb*

I extinguished my...
I extinguished the...

extracted *verb*

I extracted a\the...
I extracted my...
I extracted from my...
I extracted from the...

extricated *verb*

I extricated my...

exuded *verb*

I exuded a\the...

eye *noun*

Eyes blinked in...
Eyes closed at...
Eyes closed in...
Eyes flashed with...
Eyes narrowed against...
Eyes narrowed at...
Eyes narrowed on...
Eyes sat at...
Eyes tightened with...
Eyes turned from...
Eyes widened at...
Eyes widened in...
Eyes flew open from...
Eyes gazed down at...
Eyes peered out through...
My eye fell on...
My eye fell upon...
My eye happened on...
My eye moved on...
My eye went from...
My eyes blinked at...
My eyes bore into...
My eyes bounced between...
My eyes broke from...
My eyes closed against...
My eyes closed as...
My eyes closed for...

My eyes closed in...
My eyes closed on...
My eyes drifted across...
My eyes drifted from...
My eyes dropped in...
My eyes fell as...
My eyes fell on...
My eyes felt like...
My eyes glazed over...
My eyes landed on...
My eyes looked at...
My eyes looked like...
My eyes looked over...
My eyes moved from...
My eyes paused on...
My eyes pleaded with...
My eyes raced over...
My eyes ran on...
My eyes ran over...
My eyes remained on...
My eyes roamed from...
My eyes roamed over...
My eyes saw past...
My eyes searched for...
My eyes searched out...
My eyes skipped between...
My eyes slid over...
My eyes smiled at...
My eyes stared at...
My eyes stared into...
My eyes stayed in...
My eyes stayed on...
My eyes took in...
My eyes took on...
My eyes watered as...
My eyes went across...
My eyes went from...
My eyes went over...
The eyes sank into
The eyes stared at
The eyes took in
My eyes bore down at...

My eyes bulged out with...
My eyes darted around as...
My eyes darted around until...
My eyes flicked down for...
My eyes flicked up as...
My eyes flickered around in...
My eyes flitted down for...
My eyes glazed over at...
My eyes glinted down at...
My eyes glowed down at...
My eyes lit up at...
My eyes lit up for...
My eyes lit up with...
My eyes looked up from...
My eyes misted over as...
My eyes peered out of...
My eyes rolled around in...
My eyes rolled up in...
My eyes rolled up into...
My eyes rolled up toward...
My eyes screwed up into...
My eyes shone up at...
My eyes shot up at...
My eyes shot up from...
My eyes stared up at...
My eyes started out of...
My eyes welled up with...
My eyes went out of...
The eyes stared up at...

eyeball *noun*

My eyeballs glared out of...

eyeballed *verb*

I eyeballed my...
I eyeballed the...

eyebrow *noun*

My eyebrow rose in...
My eyebrows disappeared
beneath...

My eyebrows rose in...
My eyebrow went up in...
My eyebrows went up as...
My eyebrows went up at...
My eyebrows went up in...
My eyebrows winged up as...

eyed *verb*

I eyed a\the...
I eyed my...

eyelid *noun*

My eyelids felt like...
My eyelids flicked open as...

F

fabric *noun*
Fabric burned before...

face *noun*
Face flushed with...
Faces appeared in...
Faces floated behind...
Faces glowed in...
A face appeared at
A face hovered over
Faces gazed down at...
Faces stared up at...
My face appeared between...
My face appeared from...
My face became like...
My face blurred in...
My face blurred through...
My face broke into...
My face cleared as...
My face collapsed in...
My face collapsed into...
My face disappeared in...
My face dropped after...
My face exploded into...
My face fell as...
My face fell at...
My face fell into...
My face fell like...
My face felt like...
My face flashed before...
My face froze as...
My face glowed in...
My face glowed with...
My face hovered above...
My face hovered against...
My face hovered over...

My face lit by...
My face lit in...
My face lit on...
My face lit with...
My face looked like...
My face lowered into...
My face sagged beneath...
My face sank into...
My face slammed against...
My face stared through...
My face taunted as...
My face tightened in...
My face tightened with...
My face took on...
My face went through...
A face bobbed up out...
A face swam up at...
My face lit up as...
My face lit up with...
My face looked out at...
My face peeked out at...
My face pinched up in...
My face screwed up with...
My face swam up before...
The face lifted up toward...

faced *verb*
I faced a\the...
I faced my...
I faced down a...
I faced in the...
I faced off against my...
I faced off against the...

faded *verb*
I faded into the...
I faded out for a...

failed *verb*
I failed my...
I failed the...

I failed in my...

fainted *verb*
I fainted in a...

faintness *noun*
Faintness washed over...

faked *verb*
I faked a\an...
I faked my...
I faked out a...

faltered *verb*
I faltered at the...
I faltered for an...
I faltered in my...
I faltered in the...
I faltered to a...

fancied *verb*
I fancied the...

fang *noun*
Fangs protruded in...
Fangs sank into...
Fangs tore at...
My fangs sank in...
My fangs sank into...
My fangs surged from...
My fangs tore from...
My fangs came down on...
My fangs punched out from...
My fangs punched out into...
My fangs punched out of...
My fangs ripped out of...
My fangs sprang out of...
My fangs surged out of...

fanned *verb*

I fanned a\the...
I fanned my...
I fanned out the...

fashioned *verb*
I fashioned a...

fastened *verb*
I fastened a\the...
I fastened my...
I fastened about the...
I fastened on the...

fathered *verb*
I fathered a...

fatigue *noun*
Fatigue came on...

favored *verb*
I favored the...

favoured *verb*
I favoured my...

faxed *verb*
I faxed a...

fear *noun*
Fear believed that...
Fear blossomed in...
Fear burned through...
Fear came on...
Fear came with...
Fear churned in...
Fear closed in...
Fear coursed through...
Fear fell on...
Fear flashed through...
Fear flooded into...

Fear jolted through...
Fear jumped into...
Fear kicked in...
Fear knotted in...
Fear leapt into...
Fear lodged in...
Fear melted inside...
Fear opened in...
Fear poured through...
Fear ran like...
Fear ripped through...
Fear roared through...
Fear rolled over...
Fear rumbled through...
Fear seeped into...
Fear set in...
Fear shot through...
Fear showed in...
Fear showed on...
Fear skittered through...
Fear sliced through...
Fear stood with...
Fear streaked through...
Fear swept over...
Fear threaded through...
Fear thrilled through...
Fear thumped against...
Fear welled within...
Fear wrestled with...
My fear stank on...
My fear tore at...
My fears breathed on...

feared *verb*

I feared a\the...
I feared for my...
I feared for the...

feathered *verb*

I feathered a\the...

feature *noun*

My features sagged with...
My features swam before...
My features went from...

fed *verb*

I fed a\the...
I fed my...
I fed in the...
I fed into the...
I fed on the...

feigned *verb*

I feigned a\an...

feinted *verb*

I feinted at the...
I feinted to the...
I feinted with the...

fell *verb*

I fell the...
I fell against the...
I fell before the...
I fell behind my...
I fell behind the...
I fell beside a...
I fell down a\the...
I fell for a\the...
I fell from my...
I fell from the...
I fell in a\the...
I fell into a\an\the...
I fell into my...
I fell like a...
I fell off a\the...
I fell off my...
I fell on my...
I fell on the...
I fell onto my...
I fell onto the...

I fell over a\an\the...
I fell through a\the...
I fell to my...
I fell to the...
I fell under the...
I fell upon the...
I fell with a....
I fell down on my...
I fell down on the...
I fell out of a\the...
I fell out of my...
I fell out onto the...

felt *verb*

I felt a\an\the...
I felt my...
I felt about my...
I felt about the...
I felt above the...
I felt across my...
I felt along my...
I felt along the...
I felt around my...
I felt around the...
I felt at a\the...
I felt at my...
I felt beneath the...
I felt during the...
I felt for a\an\the...
I felt for my...
I felt in my...
I felt in the...
I felt inside my...
I felt like a\an\the...
I felt like my...
I felt on my...
I felt on the...
I felt over my...
I felt over the...
I felt through the...
I felt toward my...

I felt under the...
I felt with my...
I felt around among the...
I felt around for a\the...
I felt around for my...
I felt around on the...

fetched *verb*

I fetched a\the...
I fetched my...

fever *noun*

My fever broke at...

fiddled *verb*

I fiddled for a...
I fiddled with a\the...
I fiddled with my...

fidgeted *verb*

I fidgeted in my...
I fidgeted like the...
I fidgeted with my...
I fidgeted with the...

field *noun*

A field opened up on...

fight *noun*

The fight leaked out of...

figured *verb*

I figured a\the...
I figured my...
I figured at the...
I figured for the...
I figured into the...
I figured out a\the...
I figured with a...
I figured out from the...

filed *verb*

I filed a\an\the...
I filed my...
I filed into the...
I filed through the...
I filed up the...
I filed out of the...
I filed out with the...

filled *verb*

I filled a\an\the...
I filled my...
I filled in my...
I filled in the...
I filled out an\the...
I filled out my...
I filled up a\the...
I filled up my...

finger *noun*

Fingers brushed at...
Fingers shook as...
My finger curled around...
My finger hovered above...
My finger hovered over...
My finger rested on...
My finger slipped from...
My finger slipped over...
My finger tightened on...
My fingers bore into...
My fingers came across...
My fingers came in...
My fingers closed about...
My fingers closed around...
My fingers closed into...
My fingers closed on...
My fingers closed over...
My fingers curled around...
My fingers curled as...
My fingers curled into...

My fingers curled under...
My fingers curled underneath...
My fingers dove into...
My fingers dug at...
My fingers dug into...
My fingers felt like...
My fingers flew across...
My fingers flew over...
My fingers froze on...
My fingers groped over...
My fingers moved on...
My fingers paused in...
My fingers plunged into...
My fingers raced over...
My fingers ran across...
My fingers ran over...
My fingers sank in...
My fingers sank into...
My fingers shook around...
My fingers shook as...
My fingers shook with...
My fingers slid along...
My fingers slid beneath...
My fingers slid between...
My fingers slid inside...
My fingers slid into...
My fingers slid over...
My fingers slid through...
My fingers slipped between...
My fingers slipped from...
My fingers slipped through...
My fingers went past...
My fingers wove into...
My finger came up in...
My fingers came down for...
My fingers came out of...
My fingers came up near...
My fingers dug down beneath...
My fingers fished around on...
My fingers splayed out over...

fingered *verb*

I fingered a\the...
I fingered my...
I fingered through my...

fingernail *noun*

Fingernails dug into...
My fingernails dug into...
My fingernails sank into...

fingertip *noun*

My fingertips curled against...
My fingertips curled into...
My fingertips drifted across...
My fingertips drifted from...
My fingertips drifted over...
My fingertips ran along...
My fingertips went over...

finished *verb*

I finished a\an\the...
I finished my...
I finished around the...
I finished at the...
I finished in a...
I finished off the...
I finished out my...
I finished up a\the...
I finished up my...
I finished with a\the...
I finished with my...
I finished up in the...
I finished up with the...

fire *noun*

Fire awoke in...
Fire blazed in...
Fire burned along...
Fire burned in...
Fire burned through...
Fire came from...

Fire centered in...
Fire climbed toward...
Fire crackled in...
Fire danced along...
Fire draped around...
Fire erupted behind...
Fire erupted from...
Fire erupted in...
Fire erupted into...
Fire exploded between...
Fire exploded from...
Fire exploded in...
Fire exploded into...
Fire flashed in...
Fire flew from...
Fire glittered in...
Fire hung around...
Fire lanced across...
Fire lanced from...
Fire lanced into...
Fire leaped from...
Fire poured from...
Fire raced across...
Fire raced through...
Fire ripped through...
Fire roared into...
Fire seared across...
Fire seeped into...
Fire shot from...
Fire shot through...
Fire spiraled around...
Fire sprang from...
Fire spurted from...
Fire streamed from...
Fire symbolized by...
Fires crackled in...
Fires erupted around...
Fires raged throughout...
Fire belched out in...
Fire burned down at...
Fire erupted out of...
Fire exploded out of...

Fire ran up onto...
Fire shot out from...
Fires broke out in...
Fires spurted out of...
The fire leaped up as...
The fire licked out in...
The fire went out after...
The fire went out of...
The fires leaped up in...

fireball *noun*

The fireball soared down past...

fired *verb*

I fired a\the...
I fired my...
I fired at the...
I fired from the...
I fired off a\the...
I fired off my...
I fired through the...
I fired until the...
I fired up my...
I fired up the...

firefly *noun*

Fireflies drifted amongst...

firelight *noun*

Firelight danced across...
Firelight filtered through...
Firelight flickered across...
Firelight flickered from...
Firelight flickered in...
Firelight flickered on...
Firelight played across...
Firelight rippled along...

firework *noun*

Fireworks exploded behind...
A firework screamed up into...

firmed *verb*

I firmed my...

fish *noun*

A fish leapt out of...

fished *verb*

I fished a\an\the...
I fished my...
I fished for my...
I fished for the...
I fished in my...
I fished in the...
I fished inside my...
I fished into my...
I fished out a\the...
I fished around in a\the...
I fished around in my...

fist *noun*

Fists arrayed around...
Fists struck at...
A fist closed on
A fist slammed into
A fist thundered on
My fist rose in...
My fist traveled past...
The fist slipped through
The fist slammed down at...

fisted *verb*

I fisted a...
I fisted my...

fitted *verb*

I fitted a\the...
I fitted my...

fixed *verb*

I fixed a\the...
I fixed my...
I fixed on a\the...
I fixed up an...

flagged *verb*

I flagged down a\the...

flailed *verb*

I flailed my...
I flailed for a...
I flailed like a...

flame *noun*

Flame blossomed from...
Flame leapt in...
Flame roared from...
Flames cascaded across...
Flames leaped from...
Flames licked at...
Flames rose from...
Flames shot from...
Flame spilled out of...
Flames flared up around...
Flames licked up from...
Flames shot up in...
A flame started up inside...
The flames blazed up beside...
The flames exploded out from...

flapped *verb*

I flapped a\the...
I flapped my...
I flapped into the...
I flapped open a...

flared *verb*

I flared my...
I flared the...

flash *noun*

The flash went off as...

flashed *verb*

I flashed a\an\the...
I flashed my...
I flashed across the...
I flashed down the...
I flashed for a...
I flashed on an\the...
I flashed on my...
I flashed over the...
I flashed through a\the...

flashlight *noun*

Flashlights came on...
A flashlight went on
My flashlight bounced over...
My flashlight moved across...
The flashlight flew out of...

flattened *verb*

I flattened my...
I flattened the...
I flattened against a\the...
I flattened to my...

fled *verb*

I fled the...
I fled across the...
I fled during the...
I fled for my...
I fled into the...
I fled through the...
I fled to an\the...
I fled toward the...
I fled towards the...
I fled with the...
I fled out of a...

flesh *noun*
Flesh cut from...
Flesh fell from...
My flesh slid from...

flew *verb*
I flew a\the...
I flew my...
I flew about the...
I flew above the...
I flew across the...
I flew after my...
I flew along the...
I flew at a\the...
I flew at my...
I flew beyond the...
I flew down the...
I flew for a...
I flew in a\an\the...
I flew into a\the...
I flew like the...
I flew off a\the...
I flew off my...
I flew out the...
I flew over a\the...
I flew past the...
I flew through the...
I flew to the...
I flew towards the...
I flew up a\the...
I flew with the...
I flew down with the...
I flew on to the...
I flew out of my...
I flew out of the...
I flew up into the...

flexed *verb*
I flexed a\the...
I flexed my...

flicked *verb*
I flicked a\an\the...
I flicked my...
I flicked at the...
I flicked away my...
I flicked away the...
I flicked off my...
I flicked off the...
I flicked on a\the...
I flicked on my...
I flicked open a\the...
I flicked open my...
I flicked out the...
I flicked through a\the...
I flicked up a...

flickered *verb*
I flickered on the...

flight *noun*
The flight took off on...

flinched *verb*
I flinched a...
I flinched as a\an\the...
I flinched as my...
I flinched at my...
I flinched at the...
I flinched under the...
I flinched out of the...

flipped *verb*
I flipped a\the...
I flipped my...
I flipped off my...
I flipped off the...
I flipped on a\the...
I flipped on my...
I flipped onto my...
I flipped open a\the...
I flipped open my...

I flipped out a...
I flipped out my...
I flipped over a\the...
I flipped past a...
I flipped through a\the...
I flipped through my...
I flipped to a\the...
I flipped up my...
I flipped up the...
I flipped over beneath the...
I flipped over on my...

flirted *verb*

I flirted with a\the...

floated *verb*

I floated the...
I floated by the...
I floated in a\the...
I floated into the...
I floated like a...
I floated on a\the...
I floated past the...
I floated through the...
I floated across to the...
I floated off toward the...
I floated up in the...
I floated up toward the...

flocked *verb*

I flocked across the...

flooded *verb*

I flooded the...

floodlight *noun*

Floodlights blinked on...

floor *noun*

The floor dropped out from...

floored *verb*

I floored my...
I floored the...

flopped *verb*

I flopped my...
I flopped the...
I flopped on my...
I flopped onto a\the...
I flopped onto my...
I flopped down in the...
I flopped down on the...

floundered *verb*

I floundered my...
I floundered for an...
I floundered in the...
I floundered on the...

flowed *verb*

I flowed into the...
I flowed over the...
I flowed through the...
I flowed to my...
I flowed with the...
I flowed out of the...

flower *noun*

Flowers poured in...
Flowers swung upon...
Flowers spilled out of...

fluffed *verb*

I fluffed my...

flung *verb*

I flung a\an\the...
I flung my...
I flung down my...

I flung off my...
I flung on my...
I flung open my...
I flung open the...
I flung out a\the...
I flung out my...
I flung over my...
I flung up an...
I flung out over the...

flushed *verb*

I flushed a\an\the...
I flushed at the...
I flushed to my...

fluttered *verb*

I fluttered a...
I fluttered my...
I fluttered in the...
I fluttered like a...
I fluttered near the...

foam *noun*

Foam came from...
Foam drizzled from...
Foam dropped from...
Foam flew from...
Foam smeared against...
Foam splattered from...

focus *noun*

My focus moved from...
My focus moved off into...

focused *verb*

I focused a\the...
I focused my...
I focused on a\an\the...
I focused on my...
I focused upon my...
I focused upon the...

fog *noun*

Fog forgot about...
Fog hung across...

folded *verb*

I folded a\the...
I folded my...
I folded around the...
I folded at the...
I folded down the...
I folded in my...
I folded into the...
I folded like a...
I folded over the...
I folded up my...
I folded up the...

foliage *noun*

Foliage crunched under...

followed *verb*

I followed a\the...
I followed my...
I followed after the...
I followed as the...
I followed at a\the...
I followed behind a\the...
I followed from a...
I followed in the...
I followed up the...
I followed with my...
I followed with the...
I followed along to the...
I followed down into the...
I followed up with a\the...

fondled *verb*

I fondled the...

foot *noun*

Feet chimed in...
Feet thundered across...
A foot slammed into
My feet dug in...
My feet landed on...
My feet paused beneath...
My feet sank into...
My feet skidded along...
My feet slid from...
My feet swam in...
My feet went over...
My foot came into...
My foot crunched over...
My foot plunged through...
My foot slammed into...
My foot slammed onto...
My foot slipped onto...
My feet came out of...
My feet flew out in...
My feet flew out into...
My feet flipped out from...
My feet kicked out from...
My feet slipped out from...
My feet splayed out in...
My feet touched down on...
My feet went out from...
My foot came out of...
My foot shot out as...
My foot shot up under...
My foot touched down on...

footstep *noun*

Footsteps came behind...
Footsteps creaked behind...
Footsteps crunched in...
Footsteps echoed behind...
Footsteps sounded across...
Footsteps sounded along...
Footsteps sounded from...
Footsteps sounded on...
Footsteps splashed through...
Footsteps rang out at...

forbade *verb*

I forbade the...

forced *verb*

I forced a\an\the...
I forced my...
I forced aside the...
I forced down a\the...
I forced open the...
I forced out a\the...

forehead *noun*

My forehead rested against...
My forehead broke out in...

forged *verb*

I forged a\the...
I forged my...

forgot *verb*

I forgot a\the...
I forgot my...
I forgot about my...
I forgot about the...
I forgot for a...

fork *noun*

My fork froze in...

forked *verb*

I forked a\the...
I forked up a...

formed *verb*

I formed a\an\the...
I formed my...

forsook *verb*
I forsook the...

forwarded *verb*
I forwarded a\the...

fought *verb*
I fought a\an\the...
I fought my...
I fought against a\the...
I fought against my...
I fought amidst the...
I fought beside the...
I fought down a\an\the...
I fought down my...
I fought for a\the...
I fought for my...
I fought in a\the...
I fought inside a...
I fought like a...
I fought off a\the...
I fought on the...
I fought over the...
I fought past the...
I fought through the...
I fought to my...
I fought to the...
I fought with my...
I fought with the...

found *verb*
I found a\an\the...
I found my...
I found about the...
I found after the...
I found amongst the...
I found at a\the...
I found at my...
I found beneath the...
I found from the...
I found in a\an\the...

I found in my...
I found on the...
I found out a\the...
I found out my...
I found to my...
I found with a...
I found out about a\the...
I found out from my...
I found out on my...
I found out over the...

founded *verb*
I founded the...

fractured *verb*
I fractured my...

framed *verb*
I framed the...

freaked *verb*
I freaked about the...

freed *verb*
I freed a\the...
I freed my...

frequented *verb*
I frequented a...

fretted *verb*
I fretted in the...
I fretted with my...

fried *verb*
I fried a\the...

fright *noun*
Fright drifted through...

frightened *verb*

I frightened a...

frisked *verb*

I frisked the...

fronted *verb*

I fronted the...

frown *noun*

My frown deepened as...
My frown deepened with...

frowned *verb*

I frowned a...
I frowned after a...
I frowned as my...
I frowned as the...
I frowned at my...
I frowned at the...
I frowned for a...
I frowned in the...
I frowned into the...
I frowned out the...
I frowned toward the...
I frowned down at the...

froze *verb*

I froze an\the...
I froze my...
I froze as a...
I froze as my...
I froze at the...
I froze behind the...
I froze for a\an...
I froze in a\the...
I froze in my...
I froze like a...
I froze on an\the...
I froze with my...

I froze with the...

frustration *noun*

Frustration bled into...
Frustration foamed in...
Frustration gnawed in...
Frustration welled in...
Frustration boiled up in...
Frustration rose up in...
Frustration welled up in...
Frustration welled up inside...
My frustration came from...
My frustration came out of...
My frustration exploded out of...

fucked *verb*

I fucked a\an...
I fucked my...
I fucked up a...
I fucked up my...
I fucked up with my...

fulfilled *verb*

I fulfilled my...

fumbled *verb*

I fumbled a\the...
I fumbled my...
I fumbled about my...
I fumbled against the...
I fumbled along the...
I fumbled around my...
I fumbled around the...
I fumbled at my...
I fumbled at the...
I fumbled for a\an\the...
I fumbled for my...
I fumbled in a\the...
I fumbled in my...
I fumbled inside my...
I fumbled on the...

I fumbled open the...
I fumbled out my...
I fumbled through a...
I fumbled through my...
I fumbled under my...
I fumbled with a\the...
I fumbled with my...
I fumbled around for a\the...
I fumbled around in my...
I fumbled around in the...
I fumbled around with my...

fumed *verb*

I fumed for a...
I fumed over the...

funneled *verb*

I funneled my...
I funneled the...

furrowed *verb*

I furrowed my...

fury *noun*

Fury blazed in...
Fury blew into...
Fury burned in...
Fury burned through...
Fury coiled in...
Fury erupted through...
Fury flared in...
Fury kindled below...
Fury lashed across...
Fury rolled through...
Fury rose in...
Fury seared through...
Fury seethed in...
Fury shone from...
Fury sizzled in...
Fury stirred in...
Fury surged through...

Fury swept through...
Fury washed through...
Fury blazed out of...
Fury boiled up inside...
Fury poured out of...
Fury roared up on...
The fury went out of...

fussed *verb*

I fussed with a\the...

G

gagged *verb*

I gagged my...
I gagged against the...
I gagged as the...
I gagged on the...

gained *verb*

I gained a\an\the...
I gained my...
I gained with my...

galloped *verb*

I galloped across the...
I galloped in a...
I galloped into the...
I galloped past my...
I galloped through the...

gaped *verb*

I gaped as the...
I gaped at the...
I gaped down at the...

gasp *noun*

Gasps rang out around...
Gasps rang out as...
Gasps went up from...
Gasps went up in...
A gasp went up from...

gasped *verb*

I gasped a\the...
I gasped my...
I gasped as a\the...
I gasped as my...

I gasped at my...
I gasped at the...
I gasped from the...
I gasped in a\the...
I gasped under the...
I gasped with the...

gathered *verb*

I gathered a\the...
I gathered my...
I gathered around a\an...
I gathered at the...
I gathered behind the...
I gathered by the...
I gathered in a\the...
I gathered like a...
I gathered on the...
I gathered up a\the...
I gathered up my...
I gathered with a...

gauged *verb*

I gauged my...
I gauged the...

gave *verb*

I gave a\an\the...
I gave my...
I gave at the...
I gave off an\the...
I gave out a\the...
I gave to my...
I gave to the...
I gave up a\the...
I gave up my...
I gave in to a\the...
I gave in to my...
I gave up after a...
I gave up on the...
I gave up with a...

gawked *verb*

I gawked at the...

gaze *noun*

My gaze dipped over...
My gaze drifted across...
My gaze dropped from...
My gaze fell on...
My gaze fell over...
My gaze fell upon...
My gaze felt like...
My gaze froze on...
My gaze glanced over...
My gaze landed on...
My gaze lit on...
My gaze moved from...
My gaze moved over...
My gaze narrowed as...
My gaze narrowed on...
My gaze raked across...
My gaze ran over...
My gaze rested for...
My gaze rested on...
My gaze rested upon...
My gaze roamed over...
My gaze searched out...
My gaze skipped over...
My gaze slid across...
My gaze slid from...
My gaze slid over...
My gaze slid past...
My gaze slid toward...
My gaze slipped over...
My gaze slipped past...
My gaze stayed on...
My gaze took in...
My gaze took on...
My gaze trailed over...
My gaze traveled into...
My gaze went beyond...
My gaze went from...

My gaze went past...
My gaze went through...
My gaze drifted down for...
My gaze traveled around at...
My gaze wandered off toward...

gazed *verb*

I gazed across the...
I gazed around the...
I gazed at my...
I gazed at the...
I gazed down the...
I gazed for a...
I gazed into a\the...
I gazed into my...
I gazed out the...
I gazed over the...
I gazed past the...
I gazed through the...
I gazed toward a\the...
I gazed up the...
I gazed upon the...
I gazed around at my...
I gazed around at the...
I gazed down at my...
I gazed down at the...
I gazed off at the...
I gazed off to the...
I gazed out across the...
I gazed out at the...
I gazed out into the...
I gazed out over the...
I gazed over at the...
I gazed up as the...
I gazed up at my...
I gazed up at the...
I gazed up into my...
I gazed up through the...

gestured *verb*

I gestured a\the...

I gestured my...
I gestured across the...
I gestured after the...
I gestured around the...
I gestured at a\an\the...
I gestured at my...
I gestured behind my...
I gestured between the...
I gestured down my...
I gestured down the...
I gestured for my...
I gestured for the...
I gestured from the...
I gestured in a...
I gestured into the...
I gestured out the...
I gestured over my...
I gestured over the...
I gestured to a\an\the...
I gestured to my...
I gestured toward a\the...
I gestured toward my...
I gestured towards a\the...
I gestured up a...
I gestured with a\an\the...
I gestured with my...
I gestured around at the...
I gestured around to the...
I gestured down at my...
I gestured out into the...
I gestured out toward the...
I gestured over to a...

giggled *verb*

I giggled a...
I giggled as the...
I giggled like a...

glance *noun*

My glance came over...
My glance flickered over...
My glance flickered toward...
My glance moved over...
My glance slid from...
My glance traveled over...
My glance went from...
My glance went with...

glanced *verb*

I glanced a\the...
I glanced about the...
I glanced across the...
I glanced after the...
I glanced along the...
I glanced among the...
I glanced around my...
I glanced around the...
I glanced at a\the...
I glanced at my...
I glanced between the...
I glanced down the...
I glanced from my...
I glanced from the...
I glanced in an\the...
I glanced in my...
I glanced inside the...
I glanced into a\the...
I glanced out a\the...
I glanced out my...
I glanced out the...
I glanced outside my...
I glanced outside the...
I glanced over a\the...
I glanced over my...
I glanced past the...
I glanced through a\the...
I glanced to my...
I glanced to the...
I glanced toward my...
I glanced toward the...
I glanced towards the...
I glanced up a\the...

I glanced across at my...
I glanced across at the...
I glanced around as my...
I glanced around as the...
I glanced around at the...
I glanced around for a...
I glanced around over the...
I glanced down as my...
I glanced down as the...
I glanced down at my...
I glanced down at the...
I glanced down into the...
I glanced down toward the...
I glanced off into the...
I glanced off through the...
I glanced off to my...
I glanced off toward the...
I glanced out across the...
I glanced out at my...
I glanced out at the...
I glanced out into the...
I glanced out of my...
I glanced out of the...
I glanced out over the...
I glanced over as the...
I glanced over at my...
I glanced over at the...
I glanced over to a\the...
I glanced over to my...
I glanced over toward the...
I glanced over with a...
I glanced over with my...
I glanced up as my...
I glanced up as the...
I glanced up at my...
I glanced up at the...
I glanced up from a\the...
I glanced up from my...
I glanced up in the...
I glanced up into the...
I glanced up over my...
I glanced up through my...

I glanced up to the...
I glanced up toward the...
I glanced up with a...

glared *verb*
I glared about the...
I glared across the...
I glared around the...
I glared at a\the...
I glared at my...
I glared down my...
I glared down the...
I glared into my...
I glared over my...
I glared through the...
I glared across at the...
I glared down at my...
I glared down at the...
I glared up at the...

glass *noun*
My glass flashed at...
My glasses fell from...
My glasses fell off into...

glided *verb*
I glided my...
I glided the...
I glided into an\the...
I glided through the...
I glided to the...
I glided up the...

glimmered *verb*
I glimmered in the...

glimpsed *verb*
I glimpsed a\the...
I glimpsed my...

glistened *verb*
I glistened against the...
I glistened in the...

glittered *verb*
I glittered in the...

gloom *noun*
Gloom descended over...
Gloom hung across...
Gloom pressed in...

glove *noun*
My gloves lay on...

glowed *verb*
I glowed in the...
I glowed with a...

glower *noun*
My glower fell over...

glowered *verb*
I glowered at the...

glued *verb*
I glued my...
I glued on the...

gnawed *verb*
I gnawed a...
I gnawed on my...
I gnawed on the...

gobbled *verb*
I gobbled down my...

goggled *verb*
I goggled for a...

goosebumps *noun*
Goosebumps blossomed on...

goosed *verb*
I goosed the...

gossip *noun*
Gossip churned in...

got *verb*
I got a\an\the...
I got my...
I got around a...
I got at the...
I got behind my...
I got behind the...
I got between the...
I got down the...
I got from a\the...
I got from my...
I got in a\the...
I got in my...
I got into a\an\the...
I got into my...
I got near the...
I got off a\the...
I got off my...
I got on a\the...
I got on my...
I got onto the...
I got out a\the...
I got out my...
I got over my...
I got over the...
I got past the...
I got through my...
I got through the...
I got to a\the...
I got to my...
I got under the...

I got up a\the...
I got along with the...
I got around to the...
I got down at the...
I got down in the...
I got down into the...
I got down off my...
I got down on my...
I got down on the...
I got off at the...
I got off on a\the...
I got off to a...
I got out at the...
I got out by the...
I got out of a\an\the...
I got out of my...
I got out on the...
I got over to the...
I got through on the...
I got up during the...
I got up from my...
I got up from the...
I got up in a\the...
I got up into a...
I got up off the...
I got up on a\the...
I got up on my...
I got up while the...
I got up with a...

gouged *verb*

I gouged out my...

grabbed *verb*

I grabbed a\an\the...
I grabbed my...
I grabbed at a\the...
I grabbed at my...
I grabbed for my...
I grabbed for the...
I grabbed on the...

I grabbed onto the...
I grabbed under my...
I grabbed up a...
I grabbed up a\the...
I grabbed up my...
I grabbed on to the...

graduated *verb*

I graduated at the...
I graduated from the...
I graduated in a\the...
I graduated to a...

grappled *verb*

I grappled an\the...
I grappled at my...
I grappled for a\the...
I grappled with a...
I grappled with my...

grasp *noun*

My grasp tightened on...

grasped *verb*

I grasped a\an\the...
I grasped my...
I grasped at a\an\the...
I grasped for the...

grated *verb*

I grated my...
I grated out a...

gratitude *noun*

Gratitude surged up inside...

grazed *verb*

I grazed my...

greeted *verb*

I greeted my...
I greeted the...

greeting *noun*
Greetings exchanged with...

grenade *noun*
A grenade flew out of...
The grenade went off with...

grew *verb*
I grew a\the...
I grew in the...
I grew into a\the...
I grew up a...
I grew out of my...
I grew up among the...
I grew up as a\the...
I grew up in a\the...
I grew up on a\the...
I grew up with a\the...
I grew up with my...

grief *noun*
Grief lapped at...
Grief slammed into...
Grief snapped into...
Grief vibrated like...
Grief welled in...
The grief came on
My grief tore out of...

grieved *verb*
I grieved a\the...
I grieved for a\the...
I grieved for my...

grimaced *verb*
I grimaced as the...
I grimaced at my...

I grimaced at the...
I grimaced beneath my...
I grimaced for a...

grin *noun*
A grin broke across
A grin came over
A grin flashed in
A grin grew on
A grin stole over
A grin tugged at
My grin grew as...
My grin tightened as...
My grin widened at...
The grin bled from
The grin froze on
A grin popped up on...

grinned *verb*
I grinned a...
I grinned my...
I grinned at my...
I grinned at the...
I grinned like a\an...
I grinned out the...
I grinned through the...
I grinned around at the...

grip *noun*
My grip eased on...
My grip tightened around...
My grip tightened at...
My grip tightened in...
My grip tightened on...
The grip felt like

gripped *verb*
I gripped a\an\the...
I gripped my...
I gripped at the...

gritted *verb*
I gritted a...
I gritted my...
I gritted out between my...

groan *noun*
Groans came from...
A groan went up from...
The groan issued out of...

groaned *verb*
I groaned a...
I groaned against the...
I groaned as the...
I groaned at my...
I groaned at the...
I groaned on a...
I groaned out a...
I groaned with a\the...

groin *noun*
My groin tightened until...

groped *verb*
I groped my...
I groped the...
I groped at a\the...
I groped at my...
I groped for a\an\the...
I groped for my...
I groped in the...
I groped like a...
I groped on the...
I groped over a...
I groped toward my...
I groped with my...
I groped around for an...
I groped around in the...

ground *noun*

The ground lit up with...
The ground rushed up at...
The ground sloped down from...
The ground sloped down
towards...

ground *verb*
I ground my...
I ground the...
I ground out a\the...
I ground out my...
I ground to a...

group *noun*
The group moved off through...
The group trickled out into...

groused *verb*
I groused my...

growl *noun*
A growl rolled up from...
A growl vibrated out of...
The growl erupted out of...

growled *verb*
I growled a\the...
I growled my...
I growled at my...
I growled at the...
I growled into my...
I growled under my...
I growled with the...

grumbled *verb*
I grumbled my...
I grumbled about the...
I grumbled over my...
I grumbled through the...
I grumbled off down the...

grunted *verb*

I grunted a\an\the...
I grunted my...
I grunted as the...
I grunted from the...
I grunted in the...
I grunted like a...
I grunted through my...
I grunted under my...
I grunted with the...

guarded *verb*

I guarded my...

guessed *verb*

I guessed a\the...
I guessed my...
I guessed from the...
I guessed in the...

guided *verb*

I guided the...

guilt *noun*

Guilt ate at...
Guilt clashed with...
Guilt crowded in...
Guilt flashed in...
Guilt nagged at...
Guilt surged into...
Guilt unfurled in...

gulped *verb*

I gulped my...
I gulped the...
I gulped down a\the...
I gulped down my...
I gulped in the...

gun *noun*

A gun appeared in
A gun flew from
The gun disappeared because
The gun dropped into
The gun fell from
The gun fell on
The gun flew as
The gun landed with
The gun pointed at
The gun slipped from
A gun went off behind...
My gun jumped out of...
The gun flew out of...
The gun slipped out of...

gunfire *noun*

Gunfire came from...
Gunfire crackled in...
Gunfire echoed through...
Gunfire erupted as...
Gunfire erupted behind...
Gunfire erupted from...
Gunfire erupted over...
Gunfire exploded from...
Gunfire raged in...
Gunfire returned on...
Gunfire sizzled over...
Gunfire sounded from...
Gunfire spat from...

gunned *verb*

I gunned my...
I gunned the...

gunshot *noun*

Gunshots popped behind...
Gunshots rang out from...
A gunshot exploded out of...
A gunshot rang out with...
The gunshot rang out like...

gurgled *verb*
I gurgled my...

gut *noun*
My gut tightened as...
My gut tightened at...
My gut tightened in...
The guts fell out of...

H

hacked *verb*
I hacked as the...
I hacked at the...
I hacked into the...
I hacked out a...
I hacked through the...

hailed *verb*
I hailed a\an\the...

hair *noun*
Hair fell over...
Hair prickled behind...
Hair prickled on...
Hair stood on...
Hair came off under...
Hair flung up into...
Hair stuck up from...
My hair cascaded over...
My hair curled against...
My hair fell from...
My hair fell in...
My hair fell like...
My hair fell over...
My hair felt like...
My hair flew against...
My hair flew in...
My hair flopped across...
My hair hissed as...
My hair hung about...
My hair hung in...
My hair hung over...
My hair hung past...
My hair lay like...
My hair looked like...
My hair smelled like...

My hair stank of...
My hair stood on...
My hair tumbled over...
The hair rose along
The hair rose on
My hair billowed out in...
My hair hung down over...
My hair rayed out around...
My hair slid down around...
My hair spread out over...
My hair streamed out behind...
My hair stuck out on...
My hair stuck up at...
My hair stuck up in...
My hair tumbled down across...
The hair came out between...
The hair stood up on...
The hairs prickled up on...
The hairs stood up on...

half-expected *verb*
I half-expected the...

hall *noun*
The hall widened out into...

hallway *noun*
The hallway opened up into...

halted *verb*
I halted a...
I halted my...
I halted at a\the...
I halted before a\the...
I halted beside the...
I halted between the...
I halted by the...
I halted for a...
I halted in my...
I halted in the...
I halted on the...

hammer *noun*

The hammer smashed down
with...

hammered *verb*

I hammered a\the...
I hammered my...
I hammered into the...
I hammered on the...
I hammered upon the...

hand *noun*

Hands grabbed at...
Hands gripped in...
Hands groped for...
Hands jammed in...
Hands tightened on...
A hand closed on
A hand closed over
A hand fell on
A hand hung over
A hand landed on
A hand slapped across
A hand slipped under
Hands appeared out of...
Hands held up in...
My hand appeared over...
My hand came behind...
My hand circled over...
My hand closed about...
My hand closed around...
My hand closed into...
My hand closed of...
My hand closed on...
My hand closed over...
My hand curled around...
My hand curled into...
My hand dipped into...
My hand disappeared into...
My hand drifted across...

My hand drifted into...
My hand drifted over...
My hand dropped onto...
My hand dropped through...
My hand emerged with...
My hand faltered on...
My hand fell from...
My hand fell into...
My hand felt as...
My hand flew at...
My hand flew toward...
My hand flickered through...
My hand froze on...
My hand groped beneath...
My hand groped for...
My hand groped in...
My hand hovered by...
My hand hovered over...
My hand landed on...
My hand lay on...
My hand lowered in...
My hand meandered along...
My hand moved beneath...
My hand moved by...
My hand paused before...
My hand paused in...
My hand paused on...
My hand paused over...
My hand plunged into...
My hand rested against...
My hand rested by...
My hand rested on...
My hand rose of...
My hand rubbed at...
My hand searched around...
My hand shook around...
My hand shook as...
My hand shook at...
My hand shook inside...
My hand shook on...
My hand shook with...
My hand slid across...

My hand slid beneath...
My hand slid from...
My hand slid into...
My hand slid over...
My hand slid through...
My hand slid under...
My hand slipped behind...
My hand slipped from...
My hand slipped in...
My hand slowed in...
My hand tightened about...
My hand tightened around...
My hand tightened in...
My hand tightened into...
My hand tightened on...
My hand tightened over...
My hand wavered from...
My hand went behind...
My hand went between...
My hand went inside...
My hand went into...
My hand went over...
My hand went under...
My hand withdrew from...
My hand wove in...
My hands came beneath...
My hands came between...
My hands closed about...
My hands closed around...
My hands closed on...
My hands closed over...
My hands curled along...
My hands curled around...
My hands curled over...
My hands fell from...
My hands fell onto...
My hands felt along...
My hands felt like...
My hands flew as...
My hands flew over...
My hands flew with...
My hands flowed in...

My hands froze about...
My hands froze on...
My hands lay in...
My hands lay on...
My hands paused for...
My hands ran over...
My hands ran through...
My hands roamed as...
My hands shook against...
My hands shook as...
My hands shook despite...
My hands shook in...
My hands shook like...
My hands shook with...
My hands slid along...
My hands slid beneath...
My hands slid from...
My hands slid over...
My hands slid under...
My hands slipped from...
My hands slipped on...
My hands stayed in...
My hands stayed over...
My hands tore at...
My hands traveled over...
My hands went about...
My hands went from...
My hands went into...
My hands wove in...
The hand gestured toward
The hand hovered between
The hand lowered like
The hand tightened in
A hand came down on...
A hand came out of...
A hand shot out of...
My hand came down on...
My hand came out with...
My hand came up in...
My hand came up near...
My hand flew up as...
My hand shot out like...

My hand wandered up from...
My hands came up between...
My hands came up near...
My hands eased off of...
My hands felt around for...
My hands flew out as...
My hands went up in...
The hand shot out in...

handcuffed *verb*
I handcuffed the...

handed *verb*
I handed a\the...
I handed my...
I handed down a...
I handed out the...
I handed over a\the...
I handed over my...
I handed up the...

handgun *noun*
My handgun dug into...

handled *verb*
I handled a\the...
I handled my...

happened *verb*
I happened upon a\the...

happiness *noun*
Happiness came in...
Happiness poured through...

hardened *verb*
I hardened my...

harrumphed *verb*
I harrumphed a...

hastened *verb*
I hastened my...
I hastened along the...
I hastened down the...
I hastened into the...
I hastened to the...
I hastened up the...

hatched *verb*
I hatched the...

hated *verb*
I hated a\the...
I hated my...
I hated with a...

hatred *noun*
Hatred rose in...
Hatred seethed in...
Hatred washed through...

hauled *verb*
I hauled a\an\the...
I hauled my...
I hauled on the...
I hauled out my...
I hauled out the...
I hauled up my...

haunted *verb*
I haunted the...

havoc *noun*
Havoc reigned among...

head *noun*
Heads shook from...
Heads swiveled as...
Heads swung toward...

Heads turned as...
Heads turned at...
Heads turned from...
Heads turned toward...
My head appeared at...
My head bounced against...
My head bounced as...
My head bowed as...
My head bowed toward...
My head came above...
My head dipped in...
My head dipped toward...
My head disappeared into...
My head drooped on...
My head dropped between...
My head dropped into...
My head emerged from...
My head emerged in...
My head exploded in...
My head fell into...
My head felt like...
My head flickered in...
My head hung at...
My head hung between...
My head landed on...
My head landed with...
My head lay in...
My head lay on...
My head looked like...
My head lowered between...
My head lowered into...
My head moved as...
My head rang in...
My head rang with...
My head rested on...
My head rested over...
My head rose with...
My head searched for...
My head shook like...
My head slammed against...
My head slipped over...
My head snaked in...

My head snapped in...
My head snapped toward...
My head swam as...
My head swam with...
My head swung toward...
My head turned toward...
My head turned until...
My head wavered over...
My head went under...
My head came up at...
My head came up in...
My head came up off...
My head came up past...
My head dropped down onto...
My head popped out from...
My head popped up like...
My head slumped down onto...
My head snapped around with...
My head snapped up at...
My head snapped up from...
My head snapped up with...
My head swiveled around as...

headed *verb*

I headed a...
I headed across the...
I headed down the...
I headed for a\the...
I headed in the...
I headed into a\the...
I headed out the...
I headed over the...
I headed past the...
I headed through the...
I headed to a\the...
I headed to my...
I headed toward a\the...
I headed toward my...
I headed up the...
I headed off across the...
I headed off into the...

I headed out across the...
I headed out of the...
I headed out to the...
I headed out with a...
I headed over to a\the...
I headed up to the...

headlight *noun*

Headlights appeared on...
Headlights hurtled toward...
Headlights rose over...
Headlights shot across...
Headlights swung around...
Headlights trailed across...

healed *verb*

I healed the...
I healed of the...

heaped *verb*

I heaped my...

heard *verb*

I heard a\an\the...
I heard my...
I heard about a\the...
I heard as a...
I heard at a\the...
I heard during the...
I heard from a\an\the...
I heard in my...
I heard in the...
I heard of a\the...
I heard on the...
I heard over the...
I heard through my...
I heard through the...

heart *noun*

My heart beat like...
My heart beat with...

My heart bled with...
My heart broke as...
My heart broke at...
My heart broke for...
My heart broke into...
My heart bucked as...
My heart came near...
My heart dropped like...
My heart failed as...
My heart felt like...
My heart felt near...
My heart flipped in...
My heart jumped as...
My heart jumped at...
My heart jumped into...
My heart jumped through...
My heart lay in...
My heart leaped as...
My heart leaped in...
My heart leaped into...
My heart leaped with...
My heart leapt at...
My heart leapt in...
My heart leapt into...
My heart lurched as...
My heart lurched at...
My heart lurched in...
My heart lurched into...
My heart plummeted like...
My heart raced as...
My heart raced at...
My heart raced from...
My heart raced like...
My heart rose in...
My heart sank as...
My heart sank at...
My heart sank into...
My heart sank with...
My heart skipped at...
My heart skipped in...
My heart skipped with...
My heart slammed into...

My heart slowed as...
My heart soared like...
My heart stopped in...
My heart swelled as...
My heart swelled in...
My heart thundered in...
My heart thundered inside...
My heart tightened in...
My heart tugged at...
My heart leaped up in...
My heart lifted up in...
My heart reached out for...
My heart turned over at...
My heart turned over in...
My heart went up into...

heartbeat *noun*

My heartbeat felt like...
My heartbeat thundered against...
My heartbeat thundered in...

heat *noun*

Heat baked across...
Heat billowed past...
Heat blasted toward...
Heat bloomed across...
Heat bloomed in...
Heat bloomed inside...
Heat crept into...
Heat emanated from...
Heat erupted in...
Heat exploded on...
Heat flared in...
Heat flushed through...
Heat gusted from...
Heat ignited in...
Heat licked along...
Heat licked through...
Heat lifted into...
Heat permeated into...
Heat poured over...

Heat poured through...
Heat puddled under...
Heat raced through...
Heat radiated from...
Heat roared through...
Heat rose in...
Heat shimmered in...
Heat sizzled through...
Heat swept over...
Heat blasted out of...
Heat crept up into...
Heat roared out at...
Heat rose up from...
Heat shot out of...
Heat spread out from...
My heat spilled into...
The heat beat at
The heat broke in
The heat moved through
The heat rose in
The heat went on
The heat crept up on...
The heat radiated out of...
The heat rose up from...

heated *verb*

I heated a...
I heated up a\the...

heaved *verb*

I heaved a\an\the...
I heaved against the...
I heaved into the...
I heaved on an\the...
I heaved on my...
I heaved out a...
I heaved out a\an...
I heaved out my...

hedged *verb*

I hedged my...

I hedged on the...

heeded *verb*

I heeded the...

heel *noun*

Heels clicked across...
Heels clicked on...
My heel rang on...
My heel slipped on...
My heels dug into...
My heels rang against...
My heels sank into...

hefted *verb*

I hefted a\the...
I hefted my...

height *noun*

My height came from...

held *verb*

I held a\an\the...
I held my...
I held against the...
I held down a\the...
I held in my...
I held in the...
I held onto my...
I held onto the...
I held open a\the...
I held open my...
I held out a\an\the...
I held out my...
I held to the...
I held up a\an\the...
I held up my...
I held off on the...
I held on to my...
I heded on to the...
I held up to the...

helicopter *noun*

The helicopter took off as...
The helicopter took off from...
The helicopter went down in...

helmet *noun*

My helmet dropped with...

helped *verb*

I helped a\an\the...
I helped my...
I helped with a\the...
I helped out with a...

hesitated *verb*

I hesitated a\an\the...
I hesitated as an\the...
I hesitated at a\the...
I hesitated before the...
I hesitated between the...
I hesitated by the...
I hesitated for a...
I hesitated in my...
I hesitated in the...
I hesitated on the...
I hesitated until the...

hesitation *noun*

My hesitation felt like...

hewed *verb*

I hewed a...

hid *verb*

I hid a\the...
I hid my...
I hid at the...
I hid away my...
I hid behind a\the...

I hid behind my...
I hid beneath the...
I hid between my...
I hid by the...
I hid in a\an\the...
I hid in my...
I hid on the...
I hid while the...
I hid out in the...

highlighted *verb*

I highlighted a\the...
I highlighted my...

hiked *verb*

I hiked an...
I hiked my...
I hiked across the...
I hiked into the...
I hiked through the...
I hiked to a\the...
I hiked up my...
I hiked up the...
I hiked around for a...
I hiked out into the...
I hiked up into the...

hinted *verb*

I hinted at a...

hip *noun*

My hips rose as...
My hips surged as...

hired *verb*

I hired a\an\the...

hissed *verb*

I hissed a\the...
I hissed at the...

I hissed between my...
I hissed in a...
I hissed in my...
I hissed like a...
I hissed through my...
I hissed under my...
I hissed with the...

hit *verb*

I hit a\the...
I hit my...
I hit like a...
I hit on a\the...
I hit on my...
I hit up the...
I hit upon the...
I hit with a\an\the...

hitched *verb*

I hitched a\the...
I hitched my...
I hitched up my...

hobbled *verb*

I hobbled the...
I hobbled after a...
I hobbled down the...
I hobbled into the...
I hobbled out the...
I hobbled past the...
I hobbled to my...
I hobbled to the...
I hobbled toward the...
I hobbled up the...
I hobbled off towards the...
I hobbled out of the...
I hobbled over to my...
I hobbled over to the...

hoisted *verb*

I hoisted a\the...

I hoisted my...
I hoisted up the...

hold *noun*
My hold tightened around...

hollered *verb*
I hollered a...
I hollered down the...
I hollered out the...
I hollered toward the...

hollowed *verb*
I hollowed my...

honked *verb*
I honked the...
I honked for the...
I honked into a...

honored *verb*
I honored my...

hooded *verb*
I hooded my...

hooked *verb*
I hooked a\an\the...
I hooked my...
I hooked on my...
I hooked up the...

hooted *verb*
I hooted at an\the...

hope *noun*
Hope flared in...
Hope flared inside...
Hope flickered in...
Hope glimmered in...

Hope ignited in...
Hope leaped within...
Hope ricocheted through...
Hope rose in...
Hope shone in...
Hope slid through...
Hope soared in...
Hope soared through...
Hope strolled into...
Hope surged in...
Hope surged through...
Hope thrilled through...
Hope blazed up within...
Hope blew out like...
Hope woke up with...

hoped *verb*
I hoped a\the...
I hoped my...
I hoped for a\the...

hopelessness *noun*
Hopelessness crowded in...

hopped *verb*
I hopped a\an...
I hopped around my...
I hopped from my...
I hopped in a\the...
I hopped in my...
I hopped into a\the...
I hopped off my...
I hopped off the...
I hopped on an\the...
I hopped on my...
I hopped onto a\the...
I hopped over the...
I hopped through my...
I hopped across to my...
I hopped down from the...
I hopped down into the...

I hopped down off the...
I hopped out of the...
I hopped out with my...
I hopped over to my...
I hopped up on my...
I hopped up on the...
I hopped up onto the...

horn *noun*

Horns curled from...
Horns honked as...
Horns sounded from...
Horns vied with...
Horns blared out on...
A horn rang out behind...

horror *noun*

Horror blossomed in...
Horror came over...
Horror rolled through...
Horror swirled in...
Horror washed over...
The horror went out of...

horse *noun*

Horses grazed in...
Horses screamed in...
Horses shied on...
A horse stepped past
My horse staggered beneath...
My horse thundered on...
The horse blasted through
The horse broke into
The horse leapt into
The horse screamed as
The horse sniffed at
The horse stared at
My horse moved up behind...
My horse pulled through into...
The horse crashed down in...

hosted *verb*

I hosted a...

hour *noun*

Hours went by...

hovered *verb*

I hovered my...
I hovered the...
I hovered above the...
I hovered at the...
I hovered for a...
I hovered in the...
I hovered near the...
I hovered on the...
I hovered over the...

howled *verb*

I howled against the...
I howled inside my...
I howled out my...

huddled *verb*

I huddled against the...
I huddled at the...
I huddled behind the...
I huddled beneath the...
I huddled by my...
I huddled in a\the...
I huddled into the...
I huddled on my...
I huddled on the...
I huddled over a\the...
I huddled over my...
I huddled under my...
I huddled under the...
I huddled with my...
I huddled with the...
I huddled down in my...

huffed *verb*

I huffed a...
I huffed around the...
I huffed out a\an...

hugged *verb*

I hugged a\the...
I hugged my...
I hugged at the...
I hugged for a...

humiliated *verb*

I humiliated my...

humiliation *noun*

Humiliation burned in...

hummed *verb*

I hummed a...
I hummed my...
I hummed along with the...

humor *noun*

My humor fled as...

hunched *verb*

I hunched my...
I hunched around a...
I hunched at a\the...
I hunched beside the...
I hunched down a...
I hunched in my...
I hunched in the...
I hunched inside my...
I hunched over my...
I hunched over the...
I hunched down beside a...
I hunched down in my...
I hunched down into my...

hung *verb*

I hung a\an\the...
I hung my...
I hung against the...
I hung around a\the...
I hung around the...
I hung at a...
I hung by my...
I hung by the...
I hung for a...
I hung from the...
I hung in the...
I hung like a...
I hung near the...
I hung off the...
I hung on the...
I hung onto my...
I hung onto the...
I hung up a\the...
I hung up my...
I hung around for a...
I hung around with a...
I hung on to my...
I hung on to the...
I hung out at the...
I hung out with my...
I hung out with the...
I hung up after the...
I hung up before the...
I hung up in the...
I hung up on the...
I hung up to the...
I hung up with the...
I hung up without a...

hunger *noun*

Hunger beat at...
Hunger blazed inside...
Hunger coiled in...
Hunger coiled inside...
Hunger flared in...

Hunger gnawed at...
Hunger knotted in...
Hunger quaked through...
Hunger returned with...
Hunger ripped through...
Hunger shot through...
Hunger surged through...
Hunger tore through...
My hunger deepened with...
My hunger worked through...

hungered *verb*

I hungered for a\the...

hunkered *verb*

I hunkered behind the...
I hunkered over my...
I hunkered over the...
I hunkered with my...
I hunkered down for the...
I hunkered down in my...
I hunkered down in the...
I hunkered down into the...
I hunkered down on the...

hunted *verb*

I hunted my...
I hunted the...
I hunted down a\the...
I hunted through the...
I hunted around for my...

hurled *verb*

I hurled my...
I hurled the...

hurried *verb*

I hurried a\the...
I hurried my...
I hurried across the...
I hurried after my...

I hurried along the...
I hurried around the...
I hurried down a\the...
I hurried from the...
I hurried in the...
I hurried into a\the...
I hurried into my...
I hurried out the...
I hurried past a\the...
I hurried through a\the...
I hurried to my...
I hurried to the...
I hurried toward my...
I hurried toward the...
I hurried up a\the...
I hurried up my...
I hurried along in the...
I hurried around to the...
I hurried off down the...
I hurried off to the...
I hurried off with a...
I hurried out amongst the...
I hurried out of my...
I hurried out of the...
I hurried out to the...
I hurried over to my...
I hurried over to the...
I hurried through into the...
I hurried through to the...
I hurried up to my...
I hurried up to the...

hurt *verb*

I hurt my...

hurtled *verb*

I hurtled the...
I hurtled off the...
I hurtled through the...
I hurtled toward the...

hustled *verb*

I hustled my...
I hustled the...
I hustled across the...
I hustled down a\the...
I hustled inside the...
I hustled into my...
I hustled into the...
I hustled onto a...
I hustled out the...
I hustled past the...
I hustled to a\the...
I hustled up the...
I hustled along under the...
I hustled around to the...
I hustled out of the...
I hustled over to the...

hysteria *noun*

Hysteria clawed at...

I

ice *noun*

Ice crept through...
Ice curled around...
Ice cut through...
Ice fell like...
Ice flashed through...
Ice flowed through...
Ice formed in...
Ice glistened on...
Ice poured in...
Ice shot through...
Ice slid through...
Ice trickled into...
Ice exploded out from...

idea *noun*

Ideas ran through...

identified *verb*

I identified a\the...
I identified with the...

ignited *verb*

I ignited my...

ignored *verb*

I ignored a\the...
I ignored my...

image *noun*

Images appeared in...
Images flashed into...
Images flashed through...
Images moved beneath...
Images swelled in...

An image came up on...
The image blinked out after...
The image shimmered out of...

imagination *noun*

My imagination circled through...

imagined *verb*

I imagined a\an\the...
I imagined my...

imitated *verb*

I imitated my...
I imitated the...

impaled *verb*

I impaled the...

impatience *noun*

Impatience flashed across...
Impatience gnawed at...
Impatience simmered in...
My impatience boiled over into...

imprisoned *verb*

I imprisoned the...

inched *verb*

I inched a\the...
I inched my...
I inched across the...
I inched along the...
I inched down the...
I inched into a...
I inched through the...
I inched toward the...
I inched towards the...
I inched up the...

inclined *verb*

I inclined my...

included *verb*
I included an...
I included in the...

incomprehension *noun*
Incomprehension morphed into...

increased *verb*
I increased my...
I increased the...

indecision *noun*
Indecision rolled through...

indicated *verb*
I indicated a\an\the...
I indicated my...
I indicated for the...
I indicated in my...
I indicated to the...
I indicated with a...

indignation *noun*
Indignation flared inside...

indulged *verb*
I indulged in a...

infiltrated *verb*
I infiltrated the...

informed *verb*
I informed a\the...
I informed my...

inhaled *verb*
I inhaled a\an\the...
I inhaled my...

I inhaled above the...
I inhaled through my...
I inhaled with a...

inherited *verb*
I inherited a\the...
I inherited my...
I inherited from my...

initiated *verb*
I initiated a\the...

injected *verb*
I injected the...

injured *verb*
I injured an\the...

inquired *verb*
I inquired at the...

insect *noun*
Insects buzzed about...
Insects skittered from...
Insects swam through...

inserted *verb*
I inserted a\the...
I inserted my...
I inserted into the...

insisted *verb*
I insisted the...
I insisted on a...

inspected *verb*
I inspected my...
I inspected the...

installed *verb*

I installed a...

instinct *noun*

My instincts screamed at...
My instincts screamed for...
My instincts lit up like...

instructed *verb*

I instructed my...
I instructed the...

insulted *verb*

I insulted the...

intended *verb*

I intended the...
I intended for the...

intercepted *verb*

I intercepted the...

interrupted *verb*

I interrupted a\the...

interviewed *verb*

I interviewed a\the...

intestine *noun*

Intestines tumbled out over...

intrigue *noun*

Intrigue sparked in...

introduced *verb*

I introduced my...
I introduced the...

invented *verb*

I invented the...

invested *verb*

I invested my...
I invested the...

investigated *verb*

I investigated my...
I investigated the...
I investigated in the...

invited *verb*

I invited the...

invoked *verb*

I invoked a\the...
I invoked my...
I invoked in the...

involved *verb*

I involved my...

ire *noun*

My ire rose with...

irritation *noun*

Irritation burned through...
Irritation crept into...
Irritation flickered over...
Irritation reflected in...
Irritation simmered through...

isolation *noun*

Isolation settled in...

issued *verb*

I issued a\an\the...
I issued my...
I issued from the...

J

jabbed *verb*

I jabbed a\an\the...
I jabbed my...
I jabbed at my...
I jabbed at the...
I jabbed with a...

jacked *verb*

I jacked a\the...
I jacked my...
I jacked up my...

jacket *noun*

My jacket flew past...

jammed *verb*

I jammed a\the...
I jammed my...
I jammed on the...

jangled *verb*

I jangled my...
I jangled the...

jaw *noun*

Jaws crunched on...
My jaw dropped as...
My jaw dropped at...
My jaw hung for...
My jaw tightened as...
My jaw tightened at...
My jaw tightened in...
My jaw tightened with...
My jaw worked as...
My jaws closed on...

My jaws went for...
My jaws crunched down
through...

jealousy *noun*

Jealousy corkscrewed in...
Jealousy curdled in...
Jealousy flared in...
Jealousy mingled with...
Jealousy roiled through...
Jealousy spiked in...

jerked *verb*

I jerked a\the...
I jerked my...
I jerked against my...
I jerked as my...
I jerked at the...
I jerked in my...
I jerked into a\the...
I jerked open the...
I jerked out a\the...
I jerked to a\the...
I jerked to my...
I jerked out of my...
I jerked out of the...

jewelry *noun*

Jewelry glittered in...

jiggled *verb*

I jiggled my...
I jiggled the...

jingled *verb*

I jingled my...
I jingled the...

jogged *verb*

I jogged a\the...

I jogged at a...
I jogged down the...
I jogged in the...
I jogged on a...
I jogged to the...
I jogged toward the...
I jogged under the...
I jogged up the...
I jogged over on my...
I jogged over to my...
I jogged over to the...
I jogged up to the...

joined *verb*

I joined a\an\the...
I joined my...

jolted *verb*

I jolted my...
I jolted the...
I jolted over a...
I jolted to a...
I jolted to my...

jostled *verb*

I jostled at the...
I jostled past a...

jotted *verb*

I jotted down a\the...
I jotted down my...

judged *verb*

I judged my...
I judged the...
I judged around a...

juggled *verb*

I juggled a\the...

jugular *noun*

My jugular went in...

jumped *verb*

I jumped a\the...
I jumped about a...
I jumped across a...
I jumped as a\the...
I jumped at the...
I jumped because my...
I jumped behind a...
I jumped for the...
I jumped from a\the...
I jumped from my...
I jumped in a\the...
I jumped in my...
I jumped into my...
I jumped into the...
I jumped like a...
I jumped off a\the...
I jumped off my...
I jumped on a\the...
I jumped on my...
I jumped onto the...
I jumped over a\the...
I jumped through the...
I jumped to my...
I jumped to the...
I jumped up the...
I jumped with a...
I jumped around like a...
I jumped aside with a...
I jumped down from the...
I jumped down into the...
I jumped down off the...
I jumped out of a\the...
I jumped out of my...
I jumped up from the...
I jumped up on the...
I jumped up onto my...
I jumped up onto the...

justified *verb*

I justified my...

jutted *verb*

I jutted my...
I jutted out my...

K

keeled *verb*
I keeled over at the...

kept *verb*
I kept a\an\the...
I kept my...
I kept around my...
I kept at the...
I kept in a\the...
I kept in my...
I kept on my...
I kept on the...
I kept to my...
I kept to the...
I kept up a\an\the...
I kept up my...
I kept on to the...
I kept up on the...
I kept up with my...
I kept up with the...

key *noun*
A key fell into
My key hung from...
The key consisted of
The key sat in
The key slid into

keyed *verb*
I keyed a\an\the...
I keyed my...
I keyed in the...
I keyed on the...

kicked *verb*

I kicked a\an\the...
I kicked my...
I kicked aside a\an\the...
I kicked at a\the...
I kicked away my...
I kicked in the...
I kicked off my...
I kicked off the...
I kicked open the...
I kicked out a\the...
I kicked out my...
I kicked over the...
I kicked up my...
I kicked with my...
I kicked down from the...
I kicked out at the...
I kicked out with a...
I kicked out with my...

kidnapped *verb*
I kidnapped the...

killed *verb*
I killed a\an\the...
I killed my...
I killed for the...
I killed in the...
I killed like a...

kissed *verb*
I kissed a\an\the...
I kissed my...
I kissed by the...
I kissed for a\the...
I kissed in a\the...
I kissed on the...
I kissed up the...
I kissed with the...

knee *noun*
Knees buckled without...

My knee slammed against...
My knees collapsed beneath...
My knees dug into...

kneeled *verb*

I kneeled on my...
I kneeled on the...
I kneeled down on the...

knelt *verb*

I knelt amid the...
I knelt at the...
I knelt because my...
I knelt before a\the...
I knelt beside my...
I knelt beside the...
I knelt by my...
I knelt by the...
I knelt for a...
I knelt in the...
I knelt on my...
I knelt on the...
I knelt over a\the...
I knelt with my...
I knelt down beside the...
I knelt down in the...
I knelt down with the...

knew *verb*

I knew a\an\the...
I knew my...
I knew about a\the...
I knew about my...
I knew after the...
I knew as an\the...
I knew at a\the...
I knew because my...
I knew before the...
I knew beyond a...
I knew by the...
I knew for a...

I knew from a\the...
I knew from my...
I knew if a\the...
I knew if my...
I knew in an\the...
I knew in my...
I knew of a\the...
I knew to a\the...
I knew with a\the...
I knew without a...

knife *noun*

My knives flicked out at...
The knife dropped out of...
The knife flashed up towards...
The knife plunged down in...

knitted *verb*

I knitted my...

knocked *verb*

I knocked a\the...
I knocked my...
I knocked against the...
I knocked aside a...
I knocked at a\the...
I knocked down the...
I knocked into a...
I knocked off the...
I knocked on a\the...
I knocked out my...
I knocked out the...
I knocked over a\the...
I knocked over my...
I knocked up a...

knotted *verb*

I knotted my...
I knotted the...

knuckle *noun*

My knuckle traveled in...

knuckled *verb*
I knuckled my...
I knuckled at my...

L

labored *verb*

I labored a...
I labored on my...
I labored through a...
I labored up the...

laboured *verb*

I laboured like a...

laced *verb*

I laced my...
I laced up my...

lacked *verb*

I lacked the...

laid *verb*

I laid a\the...
I laid my...
I laid aside a...
I laid aside my...
I laid down a\the...
I laid down my...
I laid off the...
I laid on an\the...
I laid on my...
I laid out a\an\the...
I laid out my...

lamp *noun*

Lamps glowed in...

lamplight *noun*

Lamplight burned from...
Lamplight glittered on...

Lamplight glowed against...
Lamplight glowered behind...

land *noun*

The land dipped down from...
The land flattened out before...
The land opened up after...

landed *verb*

I landed a\an\the...
I landed after the...
I landed against the...
I landed amid a...
I landed amidst the...
I landed among the...
I landed at my...
I landed at the...
I landed in a\an\the...
I landed like a...
I landed near the...
I landed on a\an\the...
I landed on my...
I landed through the...
I landed upon the...
I landed with a\an...
I landed with my...

lantern *noun*

Lanterns hung from...

lapsed *verb*

I lapsed into a\an...

lash *noun*

My lashes drifted over...

lashed *verb*

I lashed my...
I lashed the...
I lashed at the...

I lashed out at my...
I lashed out at the...
I lashed out with a\the...
I lashed out with my...

lasted *verb*

I lasted a...
I lasted until the...

latched *verb*

I latched a...
I latched my...
I latched onto the...
I latched on to my...
I latched on to the...

laugh *noun*

A laugh came from
My laugh came in...
My laugh slid over...
A laugh burst out of...

laughed *verb*

I laughed a\the...
I laughed my...
I laughed around a...
I laughed as the...
I laughed at my...
I laughed at the...
I laughed for a...
I laughed from the...
I laughed if the...
I laughed in a\an...
I laughed into the...
I laughed like a...
I laughed off the...
I laughed through my...
I laughed through the...
I laughed till my...
I laughed until my...
I laughed with a\an\the...

laughter *noun*

Laughter curled from...
Laughter flickered behind...
Laughter rang through...
Laughter rippled across...
Laughter roared through...
Laughter sounded from...
Laughter spilled from...
Laughter swept through...
Laughter burst out across...
Laughter rang out over...
Laughter spread around as...
My laughter died at...
My laughter flowed over...
My laughter went on...

launched *verb*

I launched a\the...
I launched my...
I launched from the...
I launched into a\the...
I launched into my...
I launched off the...

laundry *noun*

Laundry flapped from...

lawn *noun*

A lawn swept down from...

lay *verb*

I lay a\the...
I lay my...
I lay across the...
I lay against the...
I lay among the...
I lay aside my...
I lay at a...
I lay atop my...
I lay behind the...

I lay beneath a\the...
I lay down a\the...
I lay down my...
I lay for a...
I lay in a\the...
I lay in my...
I lay like a\the...
I lay on a\the...
I lay on my...
I lay out a\the...
I lay out my...
I lay under a\the...
I lay upon the...
I lay with my...
I lay with the...
I lay around in my...
I lay down across the...
I lay down in my...
I lay down in the...
I lay down on my...
I lay down on the...
I lay down with my...

layered *verb*

I layered my...
I layered the...
I layered on the...

leaf *noun*

Leaves brushed at...
Leaves crunched beneath...
Leaves stirred around...
Leaves grew out of...
Leaves tore off in...

leafed *verb*

I leafed through a\an\the...

leaned *verb*

I leaned a\an\the...
I leaned my...

I leaned across the...
I leaned against a\an\the...
I leaned against my...
I leaned around the...
I leaned between the...
I leaned beyond the...
I leaned down a...
I leaned in a\the...
I leaned into my...
I leaned into the...
I leaned off the...
I leaned on a\an\the...
I leaned on my...
I leaned out the...
I leaned over my...
I leaned over the...
I leaned to my...
I leaned to the...
I leaned toward the...
I leaned down from the...
I leaned down so my...
I leaned in to the...
I leaned out of the...
I leaned out over the...
I leaned over on my...
I leaned over on the...
I leaned over so the...
I leaned over to the...
I leaned up in the...

leant *verb*

I leant against a\the...
I leant on the...
I leant over the...
I leant through the...
I leant upon my...
I leant out over the...

leaped *verb*

I leaped a...
I leaped across the...

I leaped at the...
I leaped atop an...
I leaped down the...
I leaped for the...
I leaped from my...
I leaped from the...
I leaped into the...
I leaped off the...
I leaped on the...
I leaped onto a\the...
I leaped onto my...
I leaped over the...
I leaped through the...
I leaped to my...
I leaped to the...
I leaped up the...
I leaped aside as a...
I leaped aside at the...
I leaped down from the...
I leaped off of the...
I leaped out of my...
I leaped out of the...
I leaped up from the...

leapt *verb*

I leapt my...
I leapt the...
I leapt across the...
I leapt after the...
I leapt at the...
I leapt between the...
I leapt down the...
I leapt for the...
I leapt from my...
I leapt from the...
I leapt in the...
I leapt into my...
I leapt into the...
I leapt off my...
I leapt off the...
I leapt on the...

I leapt over a\the...
I leapt to my...
I leapt to the...
I leapt toward my...
I leapt toward the...
I leapt up the...
I leapt on to the...
I leapt out of the...
I leapt up from the...
I leapt up into a...
I leapt up on the...
I leapt up onto the...
I leapt up to the...

learned *verb*

I learned a\an\the...
I learned my...
I learned about the...
I learned as a...
I learned at the...
I learned during my...
I learned from a\the...
I learned from my...
I learned in my...
I learned in the...
I learned of my...
I learned of the...
I learned on a\the...
I learned on my...
I learned over the...
I learned throughout the...
I learned with my...

learnt *verb*

I learnt a...
I learnt my...
I learnt as a...
I learnt from a...

leased *verb*

I leased the...

lectured *verb*

I lectured on the...

led *verb*

I led a\the...
I led my...
I led because the...
I led from the...
I led in the...
I led into the...
I led with a...
I led off between the...

leered *verb*

I leered at the...

left *verb*

I left a\an\the...
I left my...
I left about a\an...
I left after the...
I left as a...
I left at the...
I left behind the...
I left by a\the...
I left during the...
I left for a\an\the...
I left for my...
I left in a\the...
I left in my...
I left off the...
I left on a\the...
I left on my...
I left out a\an\the...
I left through a\the...
I left with a\the...
I left with my...
I left within an...
I left without a...
I left without my...

I left out of my...

leg *noun*

My leg bounced on...
My leg felt like...
My leg lay over...
My leg strengthened with...
My legs ached from...
My legs collapsed beneath...
My legs disappeared from...
My legs felt like...
My legs shook as...
My legs shook beneath...
My legs shook under...
My legs went from...
My legs went on...
My legs went over...
My legs flew out from...
My legs flew up into...
My legs shot out at...
My legs went out from...

lengthened *verb*

I lengthened my...

lessened *verb*

I lessened my...

let *verb*

I let a\the...
I let my...
I let down my...
I let off the...
I let out a\an\the...
I let out my...
I let off on the...

letter *noun*

The letter glared up at...

leveled *verb*

I leveled a\an\the...
I leveled my...
I leveled in my...

levered *verb*

I levered my...
I levered up onto my...

licked *verb*

I licked a\the...
I licked my...
I licked along a\the...
I licked at my...
I licked over the...

lied *verb*

I lied a...
I lied about my...
I lied about the...
I lied for my...
I lied in a\the...
I lied out the...
I lied to an\the...
I lied to my...

life *noun*

Life fell into...
Life flowed by...
Life lived from...
Life lived in...
Life sparked into...
A life snuffed out because...
A life spread out before...

lifted *verb*

I lifted a\an\the...
I lifted my...
I lifted from the...
I lifted off my...

I lifted off the...
I lifted onto my...
I lifted open the...
I lifted out the...
I lifted up a\the...
I lifted up my...
I lifted up from the...
I lifted up onto my...

light *noun*

Light blazed from...
Light bloomed in...
Light blossomed from...
Light broke over...
Light broke through...
Light came from...
Light cascaded behind...
Light crept into...
Light erupted as...
Light erupted from...
Light erupted in...
Light exploded from...
Light exploded in...
Light exploded inside...
Light exploded like...
Light fell across...
Light fell on...
Light filtered in...
Light filtered through...
Light flared between...
Light flared from...
Light flashed around...
Light flashed behind...
Light flickered on...
Light flowed in...
Light flowed into...
Light glimmered in...
Light glowed from...
Light ignited between...
Light kindled in...
Light lingered after...

Light played along...
Light poured from...
Light poured into...
Light radiated behind...
Light radiated from...
Light seeped through...
Light shimmered against...
Light shone from...
Light shone in...
Light shone through...
Light showed in...
Light showed through...
Light slanted in...
Light spilled from...
Light spilled into...
Light spilled over...
Light sprang in...
Light sprayed like...
Light spurted like...
Light stabbed in...
Light stabbed through...
Light streamed in...
Lights appeared in...
Lights blared across...
Lights blazed on...
Lights blinked on...
Lights came on...
Lights exploded in...
Lights flashed across...
Lights flashed in...
Lights flashed on...
Lights flickered from...
Lights flickered in...
Lights glowed from...
Lights glowed in...
Lights rigged from...
Lights showed in...
Lights spilt on...
Lights went on...
Lights winked on...
A light appeared over
A light clicked on

A light flickered in
A\the light came on...
A\the light flashed on...
A\the light went on...
Light blazed up about...
Light flooded out on...
Light poured out of...
Light spilled out of...
Light streamed down through...
My light shimmered over...
The light came through
The light continued as
The light dispersed in
The light dropped from
The light exploded in
The light fell in
The light fell on
The light flickered on
The light flowed into
The light lay on
The light leapt from
The light moved on
The light raked across
The light shimmered like
The light slammed through
The light snapped on
The light sputtered in
The light stayed behind
The light strengthened as
The light swelled around
The light went after
The light went with
A light danced around in...
The light came down from...
The light refracted off of...
The light seeped down into...
The light shot out of...
The light went off as...
The light went off in...
The light went out from...
The light went out of...
The light went out on...

The lights flickered off for...
The lights lit up in...
The lights went out as...
The lights went out for...
The lights went out on...

lightened *verb*

I lightened my...

lighter *noun*

My lighter clicked into...

lightning *noun*

Lightning ate at...
Lightning cracked behind...
Lightning crackled through...
Lightning exploded across...
Lightning exploded in...
Lightning exploded on...
Lightning fired from...
Lightning flared across...
Lightning flashed above...
Lightning flashed across...
Lightning flashed in...
Lightning flickered outside...
Lightning held in...
Lightning lanced through...
Lightning popped across...
Lightning ripped across...
Lightning ripped through...
Lightning rippled through...
Lightning sizzled through...
Lightning slashed over...
Lightning snaked along...
Lightning spilled through...
Lightning stabbed through...
Lightning streaked across...
Lightning zigged across...
Lightning zigzagged through...
Lightning crashed down from...

liked *verb*

I liked a\the...
I liked my...
I liked about the...
I liked at the...
I liked for a...

limb *noun*

My limbs felt like...

limited *verb*

I limited my...

limousine *noun*

A limousine pulled up at...

limped *verb*

I limped a\the...
I limped across the...
I limped alongside the...
I limped around my...
I limped down the...
I limped from the...
I limped into the...
I limped past the...
I limped through the...
I limped to my...
I limped to the...
I limped toward the...
I limped up the...
I limped with the...
I limped around to the...
I limped out of the...
I limped over to the...

line *noun*

The line clicked off in...
The line picked up on...
The line spread out along...
The lines came down in...

lined *verb*

I lined my...
I lined the...
I lined up the...
I lined up on the...

lingered *verb*

I lingered a...
I lingered at the...
I lingered between the...
I lingered by the...
I lingered for a...
I lingered in the...
I lingered on the...
I lingered over the...

linked *verb*

I linked an\the...
I linked my...
I linked with the...

lip *noun*

Lips parted over...
My lip curled at...
My lip curled in...
My lip curled into...
My lip curled with...
My lips broke with...
My lips closed around...
My lips closed over...
My lips curled as...
My lips curled in...
My lips curled into...
My lips curled on...
My lips curled with...
My lips drew into...
My lips flowed over...
My lips parted as...
The lips curled into
The lips went from

My lip curled up at...
My lip curled up in...
My lips came down on...
My lips drew up over...
My lips pulled down in...
My lips quirked up in...
My lips quirked up into...
My lips turned down into...

liquid *noun*

Liquid trickled from...
Liquid oozed out in...
Liquid rose up in...

listed *verb*

I listed my...
I listed the...

listened *verb*

I listened a...
I listened as my...
I listened as the...
I listened at the...
I listened for a\an\the...
I listened outside the...
I listened over a\the...
I listened through the...
I listened to a\an\the...
I listened to my...
I listened with a\an...
I listened with my...

lit *verb*

I lit a\the...
I lit my...
I lit up a...
I lit up my...
I lit up like a...
I lit up with a\the...

lived *verb*

I lived a\the...
I lived my...
I lived about a\an...
I lived above an...
I lived among the...
I lived as an...
I lived at the...
I lived behind a...
I lived by the...
I lived for a\the...
I lived in a\an\the...
I lived in my...
I lived on a\an\the...
I lived on my...
I lived through a...
I lived under the...
I lived until the...
I lived with a\the...
I lived with my...
I lived within the...
I lived out in the...

loaded *verb*

I loaded a\an\the...
I loaded my...
I loaded into the...
I loaded onto the...
I loaded up a\the...

loaned *verb*

I loaned my...

loathed *verb*

I loathed my...
I loathed the...

loathing *noun*

Loathing glittered in...

lobbed *verb*

I lobbed a...

located *verb*

I located a\the...
I located my...

locked *verb*

I locked my...
I locked the...
I locked in a...
I locked up the...
I locked on to the...
I locked up for the...

logged *verb*

I logged into my...
I logged into the...
I logged off the...
I logged onto my...
I logged onto the...
I logged off from the...
I logged on to the...
I logged out of my...
I logged out of the...

loitered *verb*

I loitered around the...
I loitered by the...
I loitered in the...

loneliness *noun*

Loneliness pressed in...

longed *verb*

I longed for a\the...
I longed for my...

longing *noun*

Longing tore at...
Longing welled like...

longsword *noun*
A longsword hung from
A longsword swung from
My longsword slid from...
The longsword crunched through

looked *verb*
I looked a\the...
I looked my...
I looked about a\the...
I looked about my...
I looked across my...
I looked across the...
I looked after the...
I looked along the...
I looked around a\the...
I looked around my...
I looked around the...
I looked as the...
I looked at a\the...
I looked at my...
I looked away a...
I looked behind the...
I looked below the...
I looked beside the...
I looked between my...
I looked beyond the...
I looked down a\an\the...
I looked down my...
I looked for a\an\the...
I looked for my...
I looked from my...
I looked from the...
I looked in a\the...
I looked in my...
I looked inside a\the...
I looked into a\an\the...
I looked into my...
I looked like a\an\the...
I looked like my...
I looked on the...

I looked out a\the...
I looked out my...
I looked out the...
I looked outside the...
I looked over a\the...
I looked over my...
I looked past my...
I looked past the...
I looked through a\the...
I looked through my...
I looked to a\the...
I looked to my...
I looked toward my...
I looked toward the...
I looked towards the...
I looked under a\the...
I looked under my...
I looked up a\the...
I looked with the...
I looked across at my...
I looked across at the...
I looked across to the...
I looked across toward the...
I looked around at a\the...
I looked around at my...
I looked around for a\the...
I looked around for my...
I looked around in a...
I looked around into the...
I looked around to my...
I looked around to the...
I looked around with a\the...
I looked around with my...
I looked beyond to the...
I looked down as my...
I looked down at a\the...
I looked down at my...
I looked down for a...
I looked down from my...
I looked down from the...
I looked down into my...
I looked down into the...

I looked down on the...
I looked down onto the...
I looked down through the...
I looked off across the...
I looked off in the...
I looked off into the...
I looked off to the...
I looked off toward the...
I looked out across the...
I looked out among the...
I looked out at my...
I looked out at the...
I looked out into the...
I looked out of my...
I looked out of the...
I looked out on the...
I looked out onto the...
I looked out over the...
I looked out through the...
I looked out toward the...
I looked out upon a...
I looked out with my...
I looked over at my...
I looked over at the...
I looked over to my...
I looked over to the...
I looked over toward the...
I looked over towards the...
I looked over with a...
I looked through to the...
I looked up after a...
I looked up as a\the...
I looked up as my...
I looked up at a\an\the...
I looked up at my...
I looked up from my...
I looked up from the...
I looked up in the...
I looked up into a\the...
I looked up over the...
I looked up through my...
I looked up through the...

I looked up to my...
I looked up to the...
I looked up toward the...
I looked up until my...
I looked up with a...

loomed *verb*

I loomed at the...

looped *verb*

I looped a\the...
I looped my...
I looped around the...

loosed *verb*

I loosed a\the...
I loosed my...

loosened *verb*

I loosened a\the...
I loosened my...

loped *verb*

I loped down the...
I loped through a...
I loped over to the...

lost *verb*

I lost a\an\the...
I lost my...
I lost at the...
I lost in the...
I lost to a\an...

lounged *verb*

I lounged against a\the...
I lounged on my...

love *noun*

The love won out for...

loved *verb*

I loved a\an\the...
I loved my...
I loved from the...
I loved in a...
I loved like a...
I loved on the...

lowered *verb*

I lowered a\the...
I lowered my...
I lowered into my...
I lowered to my...

lugged *verb*

I lugged a\the...
I lugged my...

lumbered *verb*

I lumbered out of the...
I lumbered over to my...

lung *noun*

My lungs felt like...

lunged *verb*

I lunged my...
I lunged across the...
I lunged against my...
I lunged against the...
I lunged around the...
I lunged at the...
I lunged down the...
I lunged for a\the...
I lunged for my...
I lunged in the...
I lunged into my...
I lunged through the...
I lunged to my...

I lunged to the...
I lunged toward the...
I lunged up the...
I lunged out of the...

lurched *verb*

I lurched across the...
I lurched for the...
I lurched from my...
I lurched into the...
I lurched off the...
I lurched over a\the...
I lurched to my...
I lurched over to a\the...

lurked *verb*

I lurked near the...

M

machine *noun*
Machine came at...

made *verb*
I made a\an\the...
I made my...
I made about a...
I made at the...
I made for a\the...
I made in a\an...
I made on the...
I made out a\the...
I made to a...
I made to my...
I made towards a...
I made up a\the...
I made up my...
I made with my...
I made with the...
I made out of an...
I made up on the...

madness *noun*
Madness burned in...
Madness flickered in...
The madness went out in...

magic *noun*
The magic raged out of...

mail *noun*
The mail piled up in...

maintained *verb*
I maintained a\the...
I maintained my...

malevolence *noun*
Malevolence gleamed in...

managed *verb*
I managed a\an\the...
I managed my...
I managed in a...

maneuvered *verb*
I maneuvered my...
I maneuvered the...
I maneuvered down the...
I maneuvered in the...
I maneuvered over the...
I maneuvered through the...
I maneuvered until my...

manhandled *verb*
I manhandled the...

manipulated *verb*
I manipulated my...
I manipulated the...

manned *verb*
I manned the...

manufactured *verb*
I manufactured a\the...

mapped *verb*
I mapped the...

marched *verb*
I marched the...
I marched across the...
I marched as the...
I marched down the...

I marched in a\the...
I marched into the...
I marched out the...
I marched past the...
I marched through the...
I marched to the...
I marched toward the...
I marched under the...
I marched until the...
I marched up the...
I marched off to the...
I marched out of the...
I marched over to the...
I marched up to the...

marked *verb*

I marked a\the...
I marked my...

married *verb*

I married a\an\the...
I married my...
I married into a\the...

marveled *verb*

I marveled at my...
I marveled at the...

mashed *verb*

I mashed my...
I mashed the...
I mashed out my...

masked *verb*

I masked my...

massaged *verb*

I massaged a\the...
I massaged my...

mastered *verb*

I mastered the...

matched *verb*

I matched my...
I matched the...

materialized *verb*

I materialized from the...
I materialized into a...

mattered *verb*

I mattered in a\the...

mattress *noun*

My mattress slumped against...
The mattress dipped as
The mattress landed with
The mattress lay in
The mattress sagged from

meandered *verb*

I meandered my...
I meandered down the...
I meandered through a...

meant *verb*

I meant a\an\the...
I meant my...
I meant about the...
I meant after the...
I meant in the...
I meant like the...
I meant to my...
I meant without the...

measured *verb*

I measured my...
I measured the...

meeting *noun*
The meeting broke up in...
The meeting limped along for...

melted *verb*
I melted a\the...
I melted at the...
I melted down the...
I melted into the...

memorized *verb*
I memorized the...

memory *noun*
Memories carried on...
Memories flashed through...
Memories raced through...
Memories stirred from...
A memory flashed before
A memory flickered across
A memory rose from
A memory unfolded in
Memories swirled out of...
My memory worked until...
The memory began with
The memory came at
The memory made that

mentioned *verb*
I mentioned a\the...
I mentioned my...
I mentioned at the...
I mentioned in my...
I mentioned in the...

merged *verb*
I merged my...
I merged into a...
I merged onto the...

messed *verb*
I messed up a...
I messed up my...

met *verb*
I met a\an\the...
I met my...
I met around the...
I met at a\an\the...
I met for a\an\the...
I met in a\the...
I met in my...
I met near the...
I met on an\the...
I met on my...
I met over a...
I met with a\the...
I met with my...
I met up with a...

metal *noun*
Metal clattered against...
Metal crunched around...
Metal glinted in...
Metal groaned as...
Metal raked across...
Metal rattled as...
Metal scraped on...
Metal screeched against...

midnight *noun*
Midnight slipped out of...

milled *verb*
I milled about the...

mimed *verb*
I mimed a\the...
I mimed my...
I mimed with my...

mimicked *verb*
I mimicked a\the...

mind *noun*
My mind balked at...
My mind careened through...
My mind closed around...
My mind drifted as...
My mind drifted in...
My mind flickered for...
My mind flickered over...
My mind flipped through...
My mind grappled for...
My mind raced after...
My mind raced as...
My mind raced at...
My mind raced in...
My mind raced over...
My mind raced through...
My mind raced with...
My mind ran into...
My mind ran like...
My mind ran through...
My mind screamed as...
My mind screamed in...
My mind slipped into...
My mind took in...
My mind tried over...
My mind tugged at...
My mind went into...
My mind worked in...
My mind cast out over...
My mind caught up with...
My mind lifted off in...
My mind scrabbled around like...
My mind turned down that...
My mind wandered off at...
The mind seized up with...

minded *verb*
I minded my...

minute *noun*
Minutes bled into...
Minutes crept by...

mirror *noun*
The mirror flew out of...

mirrored *verb*
I mirrored the...

mirth *noun*
Mirth shone in...
The mirth bubbled out of...

mischief *noun*
Mischief danced in...
Mischief gleamed in...

misery *noun*
Misery shone in...
Misery swam in...

misjudged *verb*
I misjudged the...

misplaced *verb*
I misplaced my...
I misplaced the...

missed *verb*
I missed a\the...
I missed my...
I missed at the...
I missed by a...
I missed for the...
I missed out the...

mist *noun*

The mist came out of...

mistook *verb*

I mistook the...

mistrusted *verb*

I mistrusted my...
I mistrusted the...

mixed *verb*

I mixed a\the...
I mixed in the...
I mixed up the...

moan *noun*

Moans drifted in...
A moan came from
My moan broke like...
A moan came out of...

moaned *verb*

I moaned a\the...
I moaned my...
I moaned about my...
I moaned around a...
I moaned as my...
I moaned as the...
I moaned at the...
I moaned like a...
I moaned with a\the...

mocked *verb*

I mocked a...
I mocked up a...

moisture *noun*

Moisture beaded at...
Moisture gleamed in...
Moisture glimmered in...
Moisture glistened in...

Moisture welled in...

moment *noun*

Moments passed that...

monitored *verb*

I monitored the...

month *noun*

Months turned into...

mood *noun*

My mood picked up at...

moon *noun*

The moon came out from...
The moon reflected up at...
The moon sailed out from...

moonlight *noun*

Moonlight filtered in...
Moonlight gleamed on...
Moonlight glinted from...
Moonlight poured in...
Moonlight poured through...
Moonlight ran like...
Moonlight shone on...
Moonlight slanted between...
Moonlight slanted through...
Moonlight spilled through...
Moonlight streamed in...
Moonlight streamed through...
Moonlight winked on...
Moonlight flooded down from...
Moonlight flooded down
through...
Moonlight shone down on...

mopped *verb*

I mopped my...

I mopped at my...
I mopped at the...
I mopped up a\the...
I mopped up with the...

morale *noun*

My morale rose as...

morning *noun*

Morning crawled toward...
Morning edged toward...
Morning passed into...
Morning slipped toward...
Morning struck with...
Morning went on...

mosquito *noun*

Mosquitoes buzzed at...
Mosquitoes lit on...

motioned *verb*

I motioned my...
I motioned the...
I motioned beside the...
I motioned down the...
I motioned for a\the...
I motioned for my...
I motioned into the...
I motioned out the...
I motioned over a...
I motioned to a\an\the...
I motioned to my...
I motioned toward a\the...
I motioned toward my...
I motioned towards the...
I motioned with my...
I motioned with the...

motored *verb*

I motored up to the...

mountain *noun*

Mountains broke in...
The mountains split off in...

mounted *verb*

I mounted my...
I mounted the...

mourned *verb*

I mourned a\the...
I mourned my...
I mourned for the...

mouth *noun*

Mouths dropped at...
Mouths opened in...
My mouth ate at...
My mouth broke into...
My mouth closed on...
My mouth closed over...
My mouth curled as...
My mouth curled in...
My mouth curled into...
My mouth descended on...
My mouth exploded with...
My mouth moved along...
My mouth moved as...
My mouth moved in...
My mouth moved like...
My mouth opened as...
My mouth opened by...
My mouth opened for...
My mouth opened in...
My mouth opened into...
My mouth opened of...
My mouth opened under...
My mouth roamed over...
My mouth slid from...
My mouth tightened against...
My mouth tightened as...
My mouth took on...

My mouth watered as...
My mouth watered at...
My mouth worked as...
My mouth worked for...
My mouth worked inside...
My mouth came down between...
My mouth came down on...
My mouth came down over...
My mouth curled up in...
My mouth curled up on...
My mouth curved up in...
My mouth lifted up at...
My mouth pulled down at...
My mouth quirked up in...
My mouth screwed up into...
My mouth tugged up at...
My mouth turned down as...
My mouth turned down into...
My mouth turned up as...

mouthed *verb*

I mouthed a\the...
I mouthed my...
I mouthed off in the...
I mouthed off to the...

moved *verb*

I moved a\an\the...
I moved my...
I moved about the...
I moved across the...
I moved along a\the...
I moved alongside the...
I moved among the...
I moved around a\the...
I moved around my...
I moved around the...
I moved aside the...
I moved at a...
I moved before the...
I moved behind a\the...

I moved below the...
I moved beyond the...
I moved down a\the...
I moved for a\the...
I moved from the...
I moved in a\the...
I moved in my...
I moved inside the...
I moved into a\the...
I moved into my...
I moved like a\an...
I moved like my...
I moved of my...
I moved off the...
I moved on the...
I moved onto the...
I moved over a\the...
I moved past a\the...
I moved through a\an\the...
I moved to a\an\the...
I moved to my...
I moved toward a\the...
I moved toward my...
I moved towards the...
I moved under the...
I moved up the...
I moved with a\the...
I moved around behind the...
I moved away from the...
I moved down into the...
I moved off because a...
I moved off to the...
I moved off toward the...
I moved on to my...
I moved on to the...
I moved out from the...
I moved out of my...
I moved out of the...
I moved over on the...
I moved over to a\the...
I moved over to my...
I moved through to the...

I moved up behind the...
I moved up into a...
I moved up to the...

movement *noun*

Movement exploded within...
Movement stirred on...

mowed *verb*

I mowed my...

mud *noun*

Mud caked on...
Mud spattered from...
Mud splashed on...
Mud squished over...
Mud flew out as...

muffled *verb*

I muffled a\the...

mulled *verb*

I mulled the...

mumbled *verb*

I mumbled a\an\the...
I mumbled my...
I mumbled as the...
I mumbled in the...
I mumbled into the...
I mumbled under my...

munched *verb*

I munched a...
I munched my...
I munched on a...
I munched on my...

murdered *verb*

I murdered a\an\the...

I murdered my...

murmured *verb*

I murmured a\an...
I murmured my...
I murmured to the...
I murmured under my...
I murmured with my...

muscle *noun*

My muscles felt like...
My muscles screamed with...

muscled *verb*

I muscled my...

mused *verb*

I mused as the...

music *noun*

Music blared from...
Music came from...
Music came on...
Music drifted in...
Music drifted on...
Music flooded in...
Music hummed in...
Music played in...
Music spilled from...
Music throbbed from...
Music floated out of...
Music floated up from...
Music spilled out of...
Music wafted down from...

mustered *verb*

I mustered a\the...
I mustered my...

muted *verb*

I muted my...
I muted the...

muttered *verb*
I muttered a\an\the...
I muttered my...
I muttered to the...
I muttered under my...

N

nagged *verb*
I nagged the...

nail *noun*
My nails dug into...

name *noun*
The name came out of...
The name screamed out in...

named *verb*
I named my...
I named the...

narrated *verb*
I narrated the...

narrowed *verb*
I narrowed a\the...
I narrowed my...
I narrowed down my...

nausea *noun*
Nausea boiled in...
Nausea hit below...
Nausea rolled over...
Nausea rose at...
Nausea rose in...
Nausea surged in...
Nausea welled in...
Nausea welled up in...
Nausea welled up inside...

navigated *verb*
I navigated the...

I navigated around a...
I navigated around my...
I navigated onto the...
I navigated to the...

neared *verb*
I neared the...

neck *noun*
My neck arched as...
My neck lay at...
My neck looked like...

need *noun*
Need coiled in...
Need resonated through...
Need surged within...
Need warred with...

needed *verb*
I needed a\an\the...
I needed my...
I needed about a...
I needed after the...
I needed at the...
I needed before my...
I needed for a\the...
I needed for my...
I needed in the...
I needed off the...
I needed out of my...

needle *noun*
The needle sprang around like...

neglected *verb*
I neglected my...
I neglected the...

negotiated *verb*

I negotiated a\the...

nerve *noun*

Nerves stirred in...
My nerves sang with...

nervousness *noun*

Nervousness radiated from...

nestled *verb*

I nestled my...
I nestled the...
I nestled on the...

neuron *noun*

My neurons screamed as...

newspaper *noun*

A newspaper flew up in...

nibbled *verb*

I nibbled a\the...
I nibbled my...
I nibbled around the...
I nibbled at a\the...
I nibbled at my...
I nibbled on my...

nicked *verb*

I nicked a...

night *noun*

Night blended into...
Night came on...
Night came upon...
Night came with...
Night closed about...
Night crashed in...
Night deepened until...
Night descended on...

Night fell in...
Night lay across...
Night thickened about...
Night came down from...
Night came down without...
The night rambled on from...
The night settled down about...

nipped *verb*

I nipped my...
I nipped at the...
I nipped on the...
I nipped up the...

nipple *noun*

My nipple slipped from...
My nipple gathered up on...

nocked *verb*

I nocked an...
I nocked my...

nodded *verb*

I nodded a\an...
I nodded my...
I nodded around the...
I nodded as the...
I nodded at a\an\the...
I nodded at my...
I nodded beyond the...
I nodded down the...
I nodded for the...
I nodded in the...
I nodded into the...
I nodded like a...
I nodded over my...
I nodded through my...
I nodded to a\an\the...
I nodded to my...
I nodded toward a\the...
I nodded towards a\the...

I nodded with a...
I nodded down at the...
I nodded out across the...
I nodded over to the...
I nodded up at the...

noise *noun*

Noise buzzed in...
Noise came from...
Noise erupted from...
A noise rustled out from...

noon *noun*

Noon rolled around...

nose *noun*

My nose closed with...
My nose looked like...
My nose rose like...
My nose rubbed against...
My nose stuffed up as...

nosed *verb*

I nosed my...
I nosed the...

nostalgia *noun*

Nostalgia rose within...

noted *verb*

I noted a\an\the...
I noted my...
I noted down the...
I noted from the...
I noted with the...

notepad *noun*

My notepad fell from...

noticed *verb*

I noticed a\an\the...
I noticed my...
I noticed about the...
I noticed along the...
I noticed for the...
I noticed in a...
I noticed inside the...
I noticed with a\an...

notified *verb*

I notified my...
I notified the...

nudged *verb*

I nudged a\the...
I nudged my...
I nudged aside a\the...
I nudged aside my...
I nudged at the...
I nudged open the...
I nudged with my...

numbered *verb*

I numbered in the...

numbness *noun*

Numbness set in...

nursed *verb*

I nursed a...
I nursed my...

nuzzled *verb*

I nuzzled my...
I nuzzled the...
I nuzzled into the...

O

obedience *noun*
Obedience hung from...

objected *verb*
I objected to the...

observed *verb*
I observed a\the...
I observed after a...

obsessed *verb*
I obsessed over the...

obtained *verb*
I obtained a\the...

occupied *verb*
I occupied my...

offered *verb*
I offered a\an\the...
I offered my...
I offered as a...
I offered up a...
I offered up my...

opened *verb*
I opened a\an\the...
I opened my...
I opened against the...
I opened on a...
I opened to a\the...
I opened up a\an\the...
I opened up my...

operated *verb*
I operated as an...
I operated under the...

opposed *verb*
I opposed the...

opted *verb*
I opted against the...
I opted for a\the...

orchestrated *verb*
I orchestrated the...

ordered *verb*
I ordered a\an\the...
I ordered my...
I ordered for the...
I ordered from the...
I ordered up a...

organized *verb*
I organized a\the...

orgasm *noun*
My orgasm crashed over...
My orgasm slammed into...
The orgasm came in
The orgasm crashed into
The orgasm went on
My orgasm roared up on...
My orgasm rolled up on...
My orgasm rushed up on...

outlined *verb*
I outlined a\the...
I outlined my...

outrage *noun*
Outrage speared through...

Outrage spiked in...
Outrage surged inside...
My outrage boiled over as...

overcame *verb*

I overcame the...

overheard *verb*

I overheard a\an\the...
I overheard my...
I overheard between the...

overlooked *verb*

I overlooked the...

oversaw *verb*

I oversaw the...

owed *verb*

I owed a\an\the...
I owed my...

owned *verb*

I owned a\the...
I owned my...
I owned for a...
I owned from my...
I owned in the...
I owned up to the...

P

pace *noun*

My pace slowed as...

paced *verb*

I paced a\the...
I paced my...
I paced about the...
I paced across the...
I paced among the...
I paced around my...
I paced around the...
I paced before the...
I paced in a...
I paced like a...
I paced off a...
I paced outside the...
I paced to the...
I paced over to the...

packed *verb*

I packed a\the...
I packed my...
I packed away a\the...
I packed in the...
I packed up my...
I packed up the...

padded *verb*

I padded across the...
I padded along the...
I padded down the...
I padded in my...
I padded into my...
I padded into the...
I padded to my...

I padded to the...
I padded toward the...
I padded up the...
I padded over to the...
I padded through to the...

paddled *verb*

I paddled after the...
I paddled toward the...
I paddled with my...

paged *verb*

I paged the...
I paged through the...

paid *verb*

I paid a\an\the...
I paid my...
I paid for a\the...
I paid for my...
I paid from my...
I paid off my...
I paid off the...
I paid on my...
I paid out the...
I paid over a...
I paid via a...
I paid with a...

pain *noun*

Pain arced like...
Pain arced through...
Pain blazed in...
Pain blossomed in...
Pain came with...
Pain crept over...
Pain drifted into...
Pain echoed through...
Pain erupted in...
Pain exploded behind...
Pain exploded in...

Pain exploded through...
Pain flared in...
Pain flared through...
Pain flashed in...
Pain flickered on...
Pain flickered through...
Pain flitted over...
Pain glittered in...
Pain jolted through...
Pain lanced at...
Pain lanced through...
Pain radiated from...
Pain ripped at...
Pain ripped through...
Pain rippled across...
Pain roared through...
Pain rocketed through...
Pain rushed along...
Pain rushed at...
Pain sank into...
Pain screamed through...
Pain seeped into...
Pain shot across...
Pain shot into...
Pain shot through...
Pain shuddered through...
Pain slashed through...
Pain sliced through...
Pain speared through...
Pain splintered into...
Pain splintered through...
Pain tore through...
Pain washed over...
The pain bore down on...
The pain dragged out for...
The pain spread out in...
The pain traveled up from...

painted *verb*

I painted a\the...
I painted my...

I painted on a...

paled *verb*

I paled a...
I paled at the...

palm *noun*

My palm landed on...
My palm rubbed against...
My palm slapped against...
My palm slid onto...
My palm slid over...
My palm slid through...
My palms dug into...
My palms broke out in...

palmed *verb*

I palmed a\an\the...
I palmed my...

panic *noun*

Panic beat inside...
Panic bloomed in...
Panic blossomed in...
Panic came upon...
Panic churned in...
Panic clamored through...
Panic clawed at...
Panic climbed in...
Panic clutched at...
Panic descended in...
Panic drilled into...
Panic exploded in...
Panic flared in...
Panic flashed across...
Panic flashed in...
Panic flooded into...
Panic flooded through...
Panic jolted through...
Panic leapt into...
Panic lodged in...

Panic raced along...
Panic raced through...
Panic ran like...
Panic ripped through...
Panic roiled in...
Panic rose in...
Panic rushed into...
Panic set in...
Panic shot through...
Panic shrieked through...
Panic sparked in...
Panic spiked in...
Panic struck like...
Panic surged in...
Panic surged through...
Panic swam like...
Panic swept through...
Panic washed through...
Panic rose up in...
Panic welled up inside...

panicked *verb*

I panicked a...
I panicked at the...
I panicked for a...

panned *verb*

I panned my...
I panned the...

pant *noun*

My pants came off in...

panted *verb*

I panted a\the...
I panted in an...
I panted to the...

pantomimed *verb*

I pantomimed the...

paper *noun*

Papers tumbled from...
Papers flew through into...

paraded *verb*

I paraded down the...

parked *verb*

I parked a\the...
I parked my...
I parked across the...
I parked around the...
I parked at a\the...
I parked behind a\the...
I parked beside the...
I parked by the...
I parked in a\the...
I parked in my...
I parked near a\the...
I parked near my...
I parked on a\the...
I parked outside a\the...
I parked outside my...
I parked under a\the...
I parked across from the...
I parked out by the...

parried *verb*

I parried a\the...

parted *verb*

I parted a\the...
I parted my...
I parted at the...
I parted before the...
I parted in the...

passage *noun*

My passage marked by...

passed *verb*

I passed a\an\the...
I passed my...
I passed across a\the...
I passed along the...
I passed away a...
I passed behind the...
I passed below the...
I passed beneath a\the...
I passed between the...
I passed by a\the...
I passed down the...
I passed from the...
I passed in a\the...
I passed in my...
I passed into the...
I passed near the...
I passed on a\the...
I passed out the...
I passed over a\an\the...
I passed over my...
I passed through a\an\the...
I passed through my...
I passed to the...
I passed under a\the...
I passed up the...
I passed out for a...
I passed out of the...
I passed out with the...
I passed through into the...
I passed through to the...

path *noun*

A path ran through
My path lay before...
The path curled on
The path wound along
The path came out on...

patrolled *verb*

I patrolled the...

patted *verb*

I patted a\an\the...
I patted my...
I patted at my...
I patted down my...
I patted for my...
I patted around in the...
I patted around under the...

pattered *verb*

I pattered a...

paused *verb*

I paused a\the...
I paused my...
I paused among the...
I paused as a\the...
I paused as my...
I paused at a\an\the...
I paused at my...
I paused before a\the...
I paused behind the...
I paused beneath the...
I paused beside a...
I paused beside my...
I paused between my...
I paused by a\the...
I paused for a\the...
I paused for my...
I paused in a\the...
I paused in my...
I paused near a\the...
I paused on a\the...
I paused on my...
I paused outside a\the...
I paused over a\the...
I paused under an...
I paused until a...
I paused upon the...
I paused with a\the...

I paused with my...

pavement *noun*
Pavement scuffed beneath...

pawed *verb*
I pawed the...
I pawed at the...
I pawed through my...
I pawed through the...

peace *noun*
Peace fell over...
Peace flowed over...

peaked *verb*
I peaked at the...
I peaked in the...

pecked *verb*
I pecked out a...
I pecked out my...

peed *verb*
I peed my...
I peed on a...

peeked *verb*
I peeked a...
I peeked my...
I peeked around a\the...
I peeked in a\the...
I peeked inside the...
I peeked into the...
I peeked out my...
I peeked out the...
I peeked over the...
I peeked through the...
I peeked under the...
I peeked out into the...

I peeked out of my...
I peeked out of the...
I peeked up over the...

peeled *verb*
I peeled a\an\the...
I peeled my...
I peeled around the...
I peeled away the...
I peeled off a\the...
I peeled off my...
I peeled open my...
I peeled open the...
I peeled out of the...

peeped *verb*
I peeped through the...

peered *verb*
I peered the...
I peered across the...
I peered after the...
I peered around the...
I peered at my...
I peered at the...
I peered between the...
I peered down the...
I peered from my...
I peered in the...
I peered inside a\the...
I peered into a\the...
I peered into my...
I peered out my...
I peered out the...
I peered over my...
I peered over the...
I peered through a\the...
I peered through my...
I peered up the...
I peered down at the...
I peered down into the...

I peered down over the...
I peered out across the...
I peered out at the...
I peered out of my...
I peered out of the...
I peered out through a\the...
I peered out toward the...
I peered up at the...
I peered up from my...
I peered up through the...
I peered up with a...

pegged *verb*

I pegged the...

pelted *verb*

I pelted across the...
I pelted over the...
I pelted up onto the...

penetrated *verb*

I penetrated the...

penned *verb*

I penned a...

perceived *verb*

I perceived the...

perched *verb*

I perched against the...
I perched at a...
I perched in the...
I perched on a\an\the...

performed *verb*

I performed a\an\the...
I performed my...
I performed at the...
I performed near the...

perfume *noun*

Perfume wafted through...

perked *verb*

I perked an...
I perked up at the...

permitted *verb*

I permitted my...

perspiration *noun*

Perspiration glistened on...

persuaded *verb*

I persuaded the...

perused *verb*

I perused the...

petted *verb*

I petted my...
I petted the...

phone *noun*

Phone buzzed in...
Phone rang at...
A phone rang from
A\the phone rang in...
A\the phone rang on...
My phone rang as...
My phone rang at...
My phone rang in...
My phone rang on...
My phone rang through...
The phone clicked in
The phone exploded into
The phone landed on
The phone rang as
The phone rang at

The phone rang beside
The phone rang during
The phone rang inside
The phone rang until
The phone rang while
The phone slipped from
The phone slipped in
The phone stood on
A phone rang out in...
My phone bounced around in...
My phone slid out of...
My phone went off with...
The phone lit up in...
The phone picked up on...

phoned *verb*

I phoned the...

photographed *verb*

I photographed the...

picked *verb*

I picked a\an\the...
I picked my...
I picked around the...
I picked at a\the...
I picked at my...
I picked from the...
I picked off a\the...
I picked off my...
I picked on the...
I picked out a\the...
I picked out my...
I picked through a\the...
I picked up a\an\the...
I picked up my...
I picked out from the...
I picked out of the...
I picked up after the...
I picked up along the...
I picked up at the...

I picked up during my...
I picked up from my...
I picked up on a\the...
I picked up with my...

picture *noun*

Pictures flashed across...
The picture cut out on...
The picture firmed up in...

pictured *verb*

I pictured a\an\the...
I pictured my...

pierced *verb*

I pierced my...

piled *verb*

I piled a\the...
I piled my...
I piled into a\the...
I piled on the...

pinched *verb*

I pinched a\the...
I pinched my...

pinky *noun*

My pinky slipped into...

pinned *verb*

I pinned a\the...
I pinned my...
I pinned up a\the...

pissed *verb*

I pissed in a...
I pissed into the...
I pissed off a\the...
I pissed on a...

pistol *noun*
The pistol fell out of...

pitched *verb*
I pitched a\the...
I pitched my...
I pitched into the...
I pitched over the...

pitied *verb*
I pitied the...

pity *noun*
Pity showed on...
Pity welled up in...

pivoted *verb*
I pivoted my...
I pivoted the...
I pivoted in my...
I pivoted off the...
I pivoted on my...
I pivoted on the...
I pivoted to my...
I pivoted toward the...
I pivoted with my...
I pivoted around in my...
I pivoted around toward the...
I pivoted around with the...

placed *verb*
I placed a\an\the...
I placed my...
I placed in my...
I placed in the...

plane *noun*
The plane leveled off at...
The plane lifted off with...
The plane swung around with...
The plane touched down in...

planned *verb*
I planned an\the...
I planned my...
I planned from the...

planted *verb*
I planted a\the...
I planted my...
I planted in the...

plastered *verb*
I plastered a\the...
I plastered on a...

played *verb*
I played a\an\the...
I played my...
I played at the...
I played for a...
I played in the...
I played on the...
I played over my...
I played with a\the...
I played with my...

pleaded *verb*
I pleaded a...
I pleaded my...
I pleaded at the...
I pleaded with the...

pleased *verb*
I pleased without the...

pleasure *noun*
Pleasure faded from...
Pleasure ran through...

Pleasure rippled through...
Pleasure rumbled through...
Pleasure rushed through...
Pleasure splintered through...
Pleasure surged through...
My pleasure came with...

pledged *verb*

I pledged my...

plodded *verb*

I plodded down the...
I plodded onto the...
I plodded through my...
I plodded up the...
I plodded out with my...

plopped *verb*

I plopped a\the...
I plopped my...
I plopped in my...
I plopped into a\the...
I plopped onto the...
I plopped down in the...
I plopped down on the...
I plopped down onto the...

plotted *verb*

I plotted a\the...
I plotted my...

plowed *verb*

I plowed my...
I plowed into the...
I plowed through a...
I plowed toward the...

plucked *verb*

I plucked a\an\the...
I plucked my...

I plucked at the...
I plucked from the...
I plucked off the...
I plucked open the...
I plucked out a\the...
I plucked out my...
I plucked up a...
I plucked up my...

plugged *verb*

I plugged a\the...
I plugged my...
I plugged in my...
I plugged in the...

plummeted *verb*

I plummeted to my...

plundered *verb*

I plundered the...

plunged *verb*

I plunged my...
I plunged the...
I plunged across the...
I plunged around the...
I plunged from the...
I plunged into the...
I plunged through a\the...
I plunged under the...

plunked *verb*

I plunked the...
I plunked down a...

pocketed *verb*

I pocketed my...
I pocketed the...

pointed *verb*

I pointed a\an\the...
I pointed my...
I pointed across my...
I pointed across the...
I pointed around the...
I pointed as the...
I pointed at a\an\the...
I pointed at my...
I pointed between my...
I pointed beyond the...
I pointed down a\the...
I pointed from the...
I pointed in the...
I pointed into the...
I pointed out a\an\the...
I pointed out my...
I pointed out the...
I pointed over my...
I pointed past the...
I pointed through the...
I pointed to a\an\the...
I pointed to my...
I pointed toward a\the...
I pointed under the...
I pointed up the...
I pointed with a\the...
I pointed with my...
I pointed down at the...
I pointed off to a...
I pointed off toward the...
I pointed out through the...
I pointed out to my...
I pointed out to the...
I pointed over to a...
I pointed up at the...
I pointed up into the...
I pointed up to the...
I pointed up toward the...

poison *noun*

Poison flooded into...

poisoned *verb*

I poisoned my...
I poisoned the...

poked *verb*

I poked a\an\the...
I poked my...
I poked around a\the...
I poked at a\the...
I poked at my...
I poked out my...
I poked through my...
I poked through the...
I poked with my...
I poked around in the...

polished *verb*

I polished the...
I polished off my...

pondered *verb*

I pondered a\the...
I pondered my...
I pondered for a...

ponytail *noun*

My ponytail swung as...
My ponytail came down past...

popped *verb*

I popped a\an\the...
I popped my...
I popped off the...
I popped on my...
I popped on the...
I popped open a\the...
I popped open my...
I popped out the...
I popped to the...

I popped up a...
I popped out of my...
I popped up inside the...
I popped up to my...

posed *verb*

I posed my...
I posed the...
I posed as a...
I posed for a...
I posed in a...

positioned *verb*

I positioned a\the...
I positioned my...

possessed *verb*

I possessed a\an\the...

posted *verb*

I posted a\the...
I posted on a...

pounded *verb*

I pounded a\the...
I pounded my...
I pounded across the...
I pounded against the...
I pounded down the...
I pounded on my...
I pounded on the...
I pounded through the...

poured *verb*

I poured a\an\the...
I poured my...
I poured along the...
I poured from the...
I poured in the...
I poured out a\the...

I poured out my...
I poured with a...

pouted *verb*

I pouted at the...

power *noun*

Power burgeoned within...
Power came from...
Power coursed through...
Power crackled between...
Power crackled through...
Power flowed from...
Power flowed through...
Power radiated from...
Power radiated off...
Power radiated through...
Power rippled through...
Power surged through...
Power thrummed through...
My power hung about...
My power joined with...
My power rode like...
My power rose up in...

powered *verb*

I powered my...
I powered the...
I powered down my...
I powered off my...
I powered off the...
I powered on my...
I powered on the...
I powered through my...
I powered through the...
I powered up the...

practiced *verb*

I practiced a\the...
I practiced my...
I practiced in my...

I practiced with a\the...

praised *verb*
I praised the...

pranced *verb*
I pranced around the...
I pranced toward the...

prayed *verb*
I prayed a\the...
I prayed my...
I prayed at the...
I prayed for a\the...
I prayed for my...
I prayed through my...
I prayed to the...

predicament *noun*
My predicament rushed in...

predicted *verb*
I predicted a...

preferred *verb*
I preferred a\the...
I preferred my...

prepared *verb*
I prepared a\an\the...
I prepared my...
I prepared for my...
I prepared for the...

presented *verb*
I presented a\the...
I presented my...

preserved *verb*
I preserved the...

pressed *verb*
I pressed a\an\the...
I pressed my...
I pressed against the...
I pressed at my...
I pressed for an...
I pressed in the...
I pressed inside the...
I pressed on the...
I pressed open the...
I pressed through the...
I pressed with my...
I pressed down on the...

pressure *noun*
Pressure amassed behind...
Pressure built on...

presumed *verb*
I presumed the...
I presumed while the...

pretended *verb*
I pretended my...
I pretended like a...

prevented *verb*
I prevented a...

pricked *verb*
I pricked a\the...
I pricked my...
I pricked up my...

pride *noun*
Pride swelled in...
Pride seemed out of...

pried *verb*

I pried a\the...
I pried my...
I pried open my...

printed *verb*

I printed a\the...
I printed out a\the...
I printed up the...
I printed out at the...

probed *verb*

I probed my...
I probed the...
I probed with my...

proceeded *verb*

I proceeded a...
I proceeded along a...
I proceeded down the...
I proceeded through the...
I proceeded to the...
I proceeded with a\the...

processed *verb*

I processed the...

prodded *verb*

I prodded a\the...
I prodded at my...
I prodded at the...

produced *verb*

I produced a\an\the...
I produced my...
I produced from my...

proffered *verb*

I proffered my...
I proffered the...

programmed *verb*

I programmed a\the...

progressed *verb*

I progressed at a...

projected *verb*

I projected a...
I projected my...

promised *verb*

I promised a\the...
I promised my...
I promised on my...

prompted *verb*

I prompted in a...

pronounced *verb*

I pronounced my...
I pronounced the...

proposed *verb*

I proposed the...

propped *verb*

I propped a\an\the...
I propped my...
I propped open the...

protected *verb*

I protected my...
I protected the...

protested *verb*

I protested a...
I protested at the...

proved *verb*

I proved my...
I proved the...

provided *verb*

I provided a\the...
I provided my...

provoked *verb*

I provoked the...

prowled *verb*

I prowled the...
I prowled along the...
I prowled beneath the...
I prowled down the...
I prowled into the...
I prowled onto the...
I prowled past the...
I prowled under the...
I prowled over to the...
I prowled up onto the...

published *verb*

I published a...

puckered *verb*

I puckered my...

puffed *verb*

I puffed a...
I puffed my...
I puffed at my...
I puffed for a...
I puffed on a\the...
I puffed on my...
I puffed out my...

pulled *verb*

I pulled a\an\the...
I pulled my...

I pulled against my...
I pulled against the...
I pulled around the...
I pulled aside a\the...
I pulled aside my...
I pulled at my...
I pulled at the...
I pulled away a\the...
I pulled down a\an\the...
I pulled down my...
I pulled from the...
I pulled in a\the...
I pulled into a\an\the...
I pulled into my...
I pulled off a\the...
I pulled off my...
I pulled on a\the...
I pulled on my...
I pulled onto a\the...
I pulled open a\the...
I pulled open my...
I pulled out a...
I pulled out a\an\the...
I pulled out my...
I pulled over a\the...
I pulled over my...
I pulled to a\the...
I pulled up a\an\the...
I pulled up my...
I pulled around to the...
I pulled in to the...
I pulled out at the...
I pulled out from the...
I pulled out into the...
I pulled out of my...
I pulled out of the...
I pulled out onto the...
I pulled over by the...
I pulled over into the...
I pulled over on the...
I pulled over onto the...
I pulled over to the...

I pulled up across the...
I pulled up alongside the...
I pulled up at the...
I pulled up behind the...
I pulled up beside the...
I pulled up in a\an\the...
I pulled up into a...
I pulled up on the...
I pulled up outside a...
I pulled up to a\the...
I pulled up to my...

pulse *noun*

A pulse traveled through
My pulse jumped in...
My pulse leaped with...
My pulse raced as...
My pulse raced beneath...
My pulse responded with...
My pulse skidded on...
My pulse skipped at...
My pulse slammed against...
My pulse stirred at...
My pulse thundered in...
My pulse raced out of...
My pulse sped up as...

pulsed *verb*

I pulsed a...

pumped *verb*

I pumped a\the...
I pumped my...

punched *verb*

I punched a\the...
I punched my...
I punched at the...
I punched in a\the...
I punched in my...
I punched off the...

I punched out a...
I punched through the...
I punched up the...

punctuated *verb*

I punctuated my...
I punctuated the...

purchased *verb*

I purchased a\an\the...
I purchased my...

purred *verb*

I purred my...
I purred like a...

pursed *verb*

I pursed my...

pursued *verb*

I pursued a\the...

pushed *verb*

I pushed a\an\the...
I pushed my...
I pushed across a\the...
I pushed against the...
I pushed aside a\the...
I pushed aside my...
I pushed at a\the...
I pushed at my...
I pushed away a\the...
I pushed away my...
I pushed by the...
I pushed down a\the...
I pushed down my...
I pushed in the...
I pushed into the...
I pushed off my...
I pushed off the...

I pushed on the...
I pushed onto my...
I pushed open a\the...
I pushed open my...
I pushed out the...
I pushed past my...
I pushed past the...
I pushed through a\the...
I pushed through my...
I pushed to my...
I pushed to the...
I pushed toward the...
I pushed up a\the...
I pushed up my...
I pushed with my...
I pushed down on the...
I pushed off into the...
I pushed off of the...
I pushed off with my...
I pushed out of my...
I pushed out of the...
I pushed out to the...
I pushed up from the...
I pushed up on my...
I pushed up onto my...
I pushed up onto the...
I pushed up to a...
I pushed up to my...
I pushed up with my...

put *verb*

I put a\an\the...
I put my...
I put aside my...
I put aside the...
I put away my...
I put away the...
I put down a\an\the...
I put down my...
I put in a\an\the...
I put in my...

I put into the...
I put off my...
I put on a\an\the...
I put on my...
I put out a\an\the...
I put out my...
I put up a\the...
I put up my...
I put out with the...
I put through at the...
I put up with a\the...

puttered *verb*

I puttered around the...
I puttered past the...

puzzled *verb*

I puzzled over the...

puzzlement *noun*

Puzzlement flashed across...
Puzzlement showed on...

Q

queried *verb*

I queried the...

question *noun*

Question asked by...
Questions died in...
Questions raced through...
Questions rose in...
Questions whirled around in...
A question sprang up in...
The question blurted out of...
The question came out in...
The question came out of...
The question exploded out of...
The question popped out of...
The question ricocheted around in...
The question seemed out of...
The questions buzzed around inside...
The questions poured out of...
The questions rolled out of...

questioned *verb*

I questioned my...
I questioned the...

quickened *verb*

I quickened my...

quiet *noun*

Quiet descended as...
Quiet descended on...
Quiet descended over...
Quiet descended until...
Quiet reigned for...
The quiet came up behind...

quieted *verb*

I quieted a...
I quieted my...

quirked *verb*

I quirked an...
I quirked my...

quit *verb*

I quit a\the...
I quit my...
I quit in the...

quivered *verb*

I quivered at the...

quoted *verb*

I quoted the...
I quoted from my...

R

raced *verb*

I raced a\the...
I raced across the...
I raced against the...
I raced along the...
I raced around the...
I raced as a...
I raced down a\the...
I raced for the...
I raced from my...
I raced from the...
I raced into the...
I raced like a...
I raced out the...
I raced past a\the...
I raced through my...
I raced through the...
I raced to the...
I raced toward the...
I raced up the...
I raced off into the...
I raced off towards the...
I raced over to the...
I raced up at an...
I raced up behind the...

racked *verb*

I racked my...
I racked the...
I racked up a...

radiated *verb*

I radiated a\an\the...

radio *noun*

My radio sputtered at...
The radio looked like

radioed *verb*

I radioed my...
I radioed in to the...

rage *noun*

Rage ate at...
Rage billowed through...
Rage blew through...
Rage boiled in...
Rage boiled within...
Rage coiled in...
Rage coursed through...
Rage exploded in...
Rage flared inside...
Rage flashed across...
Rage flashed over...
Rage flooded through...
Rage ignited in...
Rage rose in...
Rage rushed in...
Rage seared through...
Rage spiked through...
Rage steamed inside...
Rage surged through...
Rage swept through...
Rage washed over...
A rage went through
My rage swelled until...
Rage boiled up in...
Rage boiled up inside...
Rage flared up in...
Rage rose up in...
Rage welled up in...
My rage boiled over at...
The rage boiled up in...
The rage went out of...

raged *verb*

I raged at my...
I raged at the...
I raged through the...

raided *verb*

I raided my...
I raided the...

railed *verb*

I railed against the...
I railed at the...

rain *noun*

Rain blew into...
Rain clattered on...
Rain descended in...
Rain dripped from...
Rain drummed against...
Rain drummed on...
Rain fell in...
Rain fell into...
Rain fell outside...
Rain fell through...
Rain flew into...
Rain glistened on...
Rain lashed at...
Rain leaked through...
Rain passed through...
Rain pattered against...
Rain pattered on...
Rain ran into...
Rain slanted outside...
Rain washed over...
Rain beat down in...
Rain beat down on...
Rain cascaded down through...
Rain caught up with...
Rain poured down on...
The rain came down in...
The rain showed up as...

raindrop *noun*

Raindrops fell on...

raised *verb*

I raised a\an\the...
I raised my...
I raised up from my...
I raised up on my...

raked *verb*

I raked a\the...
I raked my...
I raked down a...
I raked through the...
I raked up the...

rallied *verb*

I rallied a...
I rallied my...

rambled *verb*

I rambled through the...

rammed *verb*

I rammed a\the...
I rammed my...

ran *verb*

I ran a\an\the...
I ran my...
I ran across a\the...
I ran after the...
I ran along the...
I ran around the...
I ran as a...
I ran at a\the...
I ran at my...
I ran away a...
I ran because my...
I ran behind the...

I ran between the...
I ran by the...
I ran down a\the...
I ran down my...
I ran for a\an\the...
I ran for my...
I ran from a\the...
I ran from my...
I ran in a\the...
I ran in my...
I ran into a\the...
I ran into my...
I ran like a\the...
I ran off a\the...
I ran onto the...
I ran out the...
I ran over an\the...
I ran over my...
I ran past a\the...
I ran through a\an\the...
I ran through my...
I ran to a\the...
I ran to my...
I ran toward my...
I ran toward the...
I ran towards the...
I ran under the...
I ran until my...
I ran up the...
I ran with a\the...
I ran with my...
I ran across in the...
I ran across to the...
I ran along through the...
I ran around to the...
I ran down from the...
I ran down into the...
I ran in to my...
I ran off toward the...
I ran off with a...
I ran out along the...
I ran out from the...

I ran out into the...
I ran out of my...
I ran out of the...
I ran out onto the...
I ran out to my...
I ran out to the...
I ran over to a\the...
I ran up into the...
I ran up on the...
I ran up to the...

rang *verb*

I rang my...
I rang the...
I rang for a...
I rang up the...

ranged *verb*

I ranged a...

rapped *verb*

I rapped my...
I rapped the...
I rapped at the...
I rapped on my...
I rapped on the...

rasped *verb*

I rasped a...
I rasped out a...

rat *noun*

Rats stirred from...
The rats poured out of...

rattled *verb*

I rattled my...
I rattled the...
I rattled around the...
I rattled off a\an\the...

I rattled through my...

reached *verb*

I reached a\an\the...
I reached my...
I reached above my...
I reached above the...
I reached across my...
I reached across the...
I reached around my...
I reached around the...
I reached behind a\the...
I reached behind my...
I reached beneath my...
I reached beneath the...
I reached between my...
I reached beyond the...
I reached down a...
I reached down my...
I reached for a\an\the...
I reached for my...
I reached in a\the...
I reached in my...
I reached inside my...
I reached inside the...
I reached into a\an\the...
I reached into my...
I reached like a...
I reached out a\an\the...
I reached out my...
I reached over my...
I reached over the...
I reached past the...
I reached through the...
I reached to my...
I reached to the...
I reached toward my...
I reached toward the...
I reached towards my...
I reached towards the...
I reached under my...

I reached under the...
I reached up a...
I reached up my...
I reached with my...
I reached within my...
I reached across to the...
I reached across with the...
I reached around for the...
I reached around to the...
I reached down for a\the...
I reached down for my...
I reached down inside my...
I reached down into my...
I reached down under my...
I reached down under the...
I reached down with my...
I reached out across the...
I reached out for an\the...
I reached out for my...
I reached out of my...
I reached out through the...
I reached out to a\the...
I reached out to my...
I reached out toward the...
I reached out with a\the...
I reached out with my...
I reached over for the...
I reached over to a\the...
I reached over to my...
I reached up for the...
I reached up on the...
I reached up to a\the...
I reached up to my...
I reached up with a\the...
I reached up with my...

reacted *verb*

I reacted the...
I reacted with a...

read *verb*

I read my...
I read the...
I read down the...
I read off a...
I read out my...
I read out the...
I read along with my...

readied *verb*

I readied my...
I readied the...

realised *verb*

I realised a...

reality *noun*

Reality crashed in...
Reality rushed in...
Reality wavered like...

realization *noun*

Realization broke over...
Realization dawned on...
Realization sank in...
Realization settled over...
Realization thundered into...
Realization washed over...

realized *verb*

I realized a\the...
I realized my...
I realized after the...
I realized as the...
I realized at the...
I realized for the...
I realized in an...
I realized in my...
I realized on my...
I realized with a\an...

reappeared *verb*

I reappeared a...
I reappeared after an...
I reappeared beside the...
I reappeared within a...

reared *verb*

I reared onto my...
I reared to a...
I reared up on my...

rearranged *verb*

I rearranged a\the...
I rearranged my...

reasoned *verb*

I reasoned the...

rebounded *verb*

I rebounded from the...
I rebounded off a...

rebuilt *verb*

I rebuilt the...

recalled *verb*

I recalled a\an\the...
I recalled my...
I recalled from the...

received *verb*

I received a\an\the...
I received my...
I received about the...

receiver *noun*

The receiver flew out of...

recited *verb*

I recited a\an\the...

I recited my...
I recited from the...

reclaimed *verb*

I reclaimed my...
I reclaimed the...

reclined *verb*

I reclined in my...
I reclined in the...
I reclined on an...

recognised *verb*

I recognised the...

recognized *verb*

I recognized a\an\the...
I recognized my...
I recognized as the...
I recognized from my...
I recognized from the...
I recognized in the...

recoiled *verb*

I recoiled a\an...
I recoiled at the...
I recoiled for a...
I recoiled from the...

recommended *verb*

I recommended a...

reconsidered *verb*

I reconsidered the...
I reconsidered in the...

recorded *verb*

I recorded a\the...

recounted *verb*

I recounted my...
I recounted the...
I recounted in my...

recovered *verb*

I recovered a\the...
I recovered my...
I recovered at the...
I recovered from my...
I recovered from the...
I recovered with a...

recrossed *verb*

I recrossed my...
I recrossed the...

recruited *verb*

I recruited a...

redirected *verb*

I redirected my...

redoubled *verb*

I redoubled my...

reduced *verb*

I reduced my...
I reduced the...

reeked *verb*

I reeked of the...

reeled *verb*

I reeled my...
I reeled the...
I reeled at the...
I reeled off a\the...
I reeled on my...

reentered *verb*

I reentered the...

referred *verb*

I referred to my...
I referred to the...

refilled *verb*

I refilled my...
I refilled the...

reflected *verb*

I reflected for a...
I reflected on the...
I reflected with the...

reflection *noun*

My reflection looked like...
My reflection looked out at...

refocused *verb*

I refocused my...
I refocused on the...

refreshed *verb*

I refreshed my...

refused *verb*

I refused the...
I refused on the...

regained *verb*

I regained a...
I regained my...

regarded *verb*

I regarded my...
I regarded the...

registered *verb*

I registered a\the...

I registered at the...
I registered for a\the...

regret *noun*

Regret burned in...
Regret flashed in...
Regret radiated from...

regretted *verb*

I regretted my...
I regretted the...

rehearsed *verb*

I rehearsed my...
I rehearsed the...

reined *verb*

I reined my...
I reined in my...
I reined up my...

reiterated *verb*

I reiterated my...

rejected *verb*

I rejected the...

rejoiced *verb*

I rejoiced at the...
I rejoiced in the...
I rejoiced with a...

rejoined *verb*

I rejoined my...
I rejoined the...

related *verb*

I related my...
I related the...

relaxed *verb*

I relaxed a\the...
I relaxed my...
I relaxed against the...
I relaxed at the...
I relaxed in my...
I relaxed in the...
I relaxed into a...
I relaxed on my...
I relaxed on the...
I relaxed under the...
I relaxed with a...

relayed *verb*

I relayed a\the...
I relayed my...

release *noun*

Release poured through...
Release ripped through...

released *verb*

I released a\an\the...
I released my...

relied *verb*

I relied on the...
I relied to a...
I relied upon the...

relief *noun*

Relief came in...
Relief came with...
Relief coursed through...
Relief crashed over...
Relief fell over...
Relief flared in...
Relief flashed in...
Relief flooded into...
Relief flooded through...

Relief poured over...
Relief poured through...
Relief seeped into...
Relief seeped through...
Relief showed in...
Relief showed on...
Relief spilled over...
Relief spilled through...
Relief swamped over...
Relief swelled in...
Relief swept over...
Relief swept through...
Relief washed over...
Relief washed through...
Relief went through...
My relief came with...
Relief sighed out of...

relinquished *verb*

I relinquished my...

relished *verb*

I relished the...

relived *verb*

I relived the...

remained *verb*

I remained a\an\the...
I remained at my...
I remained at the...
I remained by the...
I remained for an...
I remained in a\the...
I remained in my...
I remained on my...
I remained on the...
I remained outside the...
I remained to the...
I remained with the...

remarked *verb*

I remarked of the...

remarried *verb*

I remarried a...

remembered *verb*

I remembered a\an\the...
I remembered my...
I remembered about the...
I remembered as a...
I remembered for a...
I remembered from a\an\the...
I remembered from my...
I remembered of my...
I remembered with an...

reminded *verb*

I reminded my...
I reminded the...

removed *verb*

I removed a\the...
I removed my...

renewed *verb*

I renewed my...

rent *verb*

I rent a\the...

rented *verb*

I rented a\an\the...
I rented my...

reopened *verb*

I reopened a\the...

repaired *verb*

I repaired my...

I repaired the...

repeated *verb*

I repeated my...
I repeated the...
I repeated under my...
I repeated with an...

replaced *verb*

I replaced my...
I replaced the...

replayed *verb*

I replayed my...
I replayed the...
I replayed in my...

replied *verb*

I replied in a\the...
I replied through the...
I replied to my...
I replied to the...
I replied with a\the...

reply *noun*

My reply came with...
My reply landed like...
The reply came from
The reply came in
The reply came with
The reply came within
My reply exploded out of...
The reply shot out of...

report *noun*

The report traveled off in...

reported *verb*

I reported my...
I reported the...

I reported on the...
I reported to a\the...

repositioned *verb*

I repositioned my...

represented *verb*

I represented a\the...

repulsion *noun*

Repulsion ripped through...

requested *verb*

I requested a\the...

required *verb*

I required a...

reread *verb*

I reread a\the...
I reread my...

rescued *verb*

I rescued a\the...
I rescued from the...

researched *verb*

I researched my...
I researched the...

resembled *verb*

I resembled a...

resented *verb*

I resented my...
I resented the...

reserved *verb*

I reserved the...

resignation *noun*

Resignation bled into...

resigned *verb*

I resigned my...
I resigned from my...
I resigned from the...

resisted *verb*

I resisted a\an\the...
I resisted my...
I resisted for a\the...
I resisted until the...

resolution *noun*

My resolution grew as...

resolved *verb*

I resolved my...

respected *verb*

I respected the...

responded *verb*

I responded to a\the...
I responded with a\an...
I responded with my...

rest *noun*

The rest came out in...
The rest moved off without...

rested *verb*

I rested a\an\the...
I rested my...
I rested against an...
I rested for a\an...
I rested in the...
I rested on a\the...

I rested on my...
I rested throughout the...
I rested with my...

restlessness *noun*

A restlessness took over from...

restored *verb*

I restored the...

restrained *verb*

I restrained a\an\the...

resumed *verb*

I resumed my...
I resumed with a...

retained *verb*

I retained from the...

retaliated *verb*

I retaliated with a...

retched *verb*

I retched until my...
I retched on to the...

retired *verb*

I retired my...
I retired the...
I retired from the...
I retired through the...
I retired to my...

retraced *verb*

I retraced my...
I retraced the...
I retraced in my...

retracted *verb*

I retracted my...
I retracted the...

retreated *verb*

I retreated a\the...
I retreated behind a...
I retreated from the...
I retreated into an\the...
I retreated into my...
I retreated to a\the...
I retreated to my...
I retreated until my...

retrieved *verb*

I retrieved a\an\the...
I retrieved my...

returned *verb*

I returned a\an\the...
I returned my...
I returned after a...
I returned as a...
I returned for the...
I returned from my...
I returned from the...
I returned in a...
I returned on the...
I returned through the...
I returned to a\the...
I returned to my...
I returned with a\the...
I returned within the...

revealed *verb*

I revealed my...
I revealed the...

reveled *verb*

I reveled in the...

revenge *noun*
Revenge flashed through...

reverence *noun*
Reverence found that...
Reverence strode towards...

reversed *verb*
I reversed my...
I reversed the...
I reversed into a...
I reversed on the...

reviewed *verb*
I reviewed my...
I reviewed the...

revulsion *noun*
Revulsion roiled like...
My revulsion tore through...

revved *verb*
I revved the...
I revved up the...

rewarded *verb*
I rewarded the...

rewound *verb*
I rewound my...
I rewound the...

rib *noun*
My ribs felt like...
My ribs sank as...
Ribs poked out of...

ricochet *noun*
Ricochets bounced around...

riffled *verb*
I riffled the...
I riffled through the...

rifled *verb*
I rifled the...
I rifled through my...
I rifled through the...

rigged *verb*
I rigged a\the...
I rigged up in the...

righted *verb*
I righted the...

rinsed *verb*
I rinsed my...
I rinsed the...
I rinsed away the...
I rinsed off the...
I rinsed out my...
I rinsed out the...

ripped *verb*
I ripped a\the...
I ripped my...
I ripped at my...
I ripped at the...
I ripped away the...
I ripped into the...
I ripped off a\the...
I ripped off my...
I ripped open a\the...
I ripped out the...

rippled *verb*
I rippled from the...

risked *verb*

I risked a\the...
I risked my...

river *noun*

The river rushed up in...
The river sluiced out from...

road *noun*

The road dipped down toward...
The road flattened out at...

roamed *verb*

I roamed the...
I roamed around the...
I roamed through the...

roar *noun*

A roar clawed up from...
A roar went up as...
A roar went up at...
A roar went up from...

roared *verb*

I roared a\the...
I roared my...
I roared as the...
I roared at the...
I roared down the...
I roared for the...
I roared in the...
I roared into the...
I roared like an...
I roared out my...
I roared over a...
I roared past a...
I roared past my...
I roared through the...
I roared toward the...
I roared until my...
I roared with the...
I roared out of the...

robbed *verb*

I robbed a\the...

rock *noun*

Rocks loomed out of...
The rocks hailed down around...

rocked *verb*

I rocked a\the...
I rocked my...
I rocked for a...
I rocked in the...
I rocked on my...
I rocked onto my...
I rocked onto the...
I rocked to a...
I rocked to my...
I rocked with the...
I rocked up on my...

rocketed *verb*

I rocketed by the...
I rocketed into the...

rode *verb*

I rode a\the...
I rode my...
I rode along the...
I rode at a\the...
I rode beside the...
I rode between the...
I rode for a\the...
I rode in a\the...
I rode inside the...
I rode into a\the...
I rode like a...
I rode near the...
I rode on a...
I rode out the...
I rode past a...

I rode through the...
I rode to the...
I rode toward the...
I rode up the...
I rode with a\the...
I rode with my...
I rode along for a...
I rode down in the...
I rode down on the...
I rode out of the...
I rode up in the...
I rode up to the...
I rode up with a...

rolled *verb*

I rolled a\the...
I rolled my...
I rolled across the...
I rolled behind a...
I rolled down my...
I rolled down the...
I rolled from my...
I rolled in a\the...
I rolled in my...
I rolled into a\the...
I rolled off my...
I rolled off the...
I rolled on my...
I rolled on the...
I rolled onto my...
I rolled onto the...
I rolled out a...
I rolled over the...
I rolled past the...
I rolled through the...
I rolled to a\the...
I rolled to my...
I rolled toward my...
I rolled under the...
I rolled up a\the...
I rolled up my...

I rolled with the...
I rolled around in the...
I rolled aside as the...
I rolled on to my...
I rolled out of the...
I rolled out onto the...
I rolled over in the...
I rolled over on my...
I rolled over on the...
I rolled over onto my...
I rolled over to my...
I rolled up at the...
I rolled up in a...
I rolled up to my...

room *noun*

My room looked over...
My room opened on...
The room brimmed with
The room bristled with
The room came into
The room erupted in
The room erupted into
The room erupted with
The room exploded in
The room exploded into
The room exploded with
The room fell into
The room flickered with
The room leapt into
The room lit behind
The room looked like
The room plunged into
The room rang in
The room rang with
The room rose in
The room shook as
The room shook in
The room smelled like
The room smelled of
The room stank like

The room stank of
The room swam in
The room breathed out as...
The room lit up in...
The room lit up with...

rooted *verb*

I rooted for the...
I rooted in my...
I rooted in the...
I rooted through my...
I rooted through the...
I rooted around for my...
I rooted around in the...

rope *noun*

Ropes hung from...

rose *verb*

I rose the...
I rose above the...
I rose after a...
I rose at the...
I rose before the...
I rose behind the...
I rose from a\the...
I rose from my...
I rose in a\the...
I rose into the...
I rose like a\the...
I rose on my...
I rose onto my...
I rose onto the...
I rose through the...
I rose to my...
I rose to the...
I rose under the...
I rose until my...
I rose with a\an\the...
I rose out of my...
I rose up on my...

I rose up on the...
I rose up to my...

rotated *verb*

I rotated my...
I rotated the...
I rotated to the...

rounded *verb*

I rounded a\the...
I rounded my...
I rounded on my...
I rounded on the...
I rounded to the...
I rounded toward the...

roused *verb*

I roused a\the...

route *noun*

The route wound up into...

rowed *verb*

I rowed a...
I rowed in the...

rubbed *verb*

I rubbed a\an\the...
I rubbed my...
I rubbed along the...
I rubbed at a\the...
I rubbed at my...
I rubbed out my...
I rubbed over my...

ruffled *verb*

I ruffled my...
I ruffled the...

ruined *verb*

I ruined a\the...
I ruined my...

ruled *verb*

I ruled my...
I ruled the...
I ruled against the...
I ruled from the...

rumbled *verb*

I rumbled a...
I rumbled out my...
I rumbled over the...
I rumbled through a...
I rumbled up the...
I rumbled with a...

rummaged *verb*

I rummaged my...
I rummaged the...
I rummaged among the...
I rummaged in a\the...
I rummaged in my...
I rummaged out my...
I rummaged through a\the...
I rummaged through my...
I rummaged under the...
I rummaged around in my...
I rummaged around in the...
I rummaged through while my...

rumor *noun*

Rumors abounded about...
Rumors existed that...

rumour *noun*

Rumours said that...

rushed *verb*

I rushed the...

I rushed across the...
I rushed around the...
I rushed at the...
I rushed down the...
I rushed for the...
I rushed from the...
I rushed in a...
I rushed into a\the...
I rushed off the...
I rushed out the...
I rushed past a\the...
I rushed through the...
I rushed to my...
I rushed to the...
I rushed toward the...
I rushed towards the...
I rushed up the...
I rushed around to the...
I rushed off down a...
I rushed out into the...
I rushed out of the...
I rushed over to the...
I rushed through to the...

S

sacrificed *verb*

I sacrificed a...
I sacrificed my...

saddled *verb*

I saddled my...

sadness *noun*

Sadness bled into...
Sadness lived in...

sagged *verb*

I sagged against a\the...
I sagged against my...
I sagged at the...
I sagged into my...
I sagged into the...
I sagged onto my...
I sagged onto the...
I sagged down against the...

said *verb*

I said a\an\the...
I said my...
I said about a\an\the...
I said after a\the...
I said around a\the...
I said as a\the...
I said at the...
I said before the...
I said between my...
I said for the...
I said from my...
I said from the...
I said if the...
I said in a\an\the...
I said in my...
I said into a\the...
I said like a...
I said off the...
I said on a\the...
I said over a\the...
I said over my...
I said through a...
I said through my...
I said to a\an\the...
I said to my...
I said under my...
I said with a\an\the...
I said with my...
I said without a...
I said out of the...

sailboat *noun*

Sailboats tacked into...

sailed *verb*

I sailed a\the...
I sailed aboard a...
I sailed across the...
I sailed by the...
I sailed into the...
I sailed like a...
I sailed through the...
I sailed up the...

salted *verb*

I salted the...

saluted *verb*

I saluted the...
I saluted from the...
I saluted with a\the...

sang *verb*

I sang a\the...

I sang my...
I sang for my...
I sang in a\the...
I sang like a...
I sang of my...
I sang of the...
I sang through the...
I sang to my...
I sang with the...
I sang along with the...

sank *verb*

I sank my...
I sank the...
I sank into a\an\the...
I sank into my...
I sank onto a\the...
I sank to my...
I sank to the...
I sank under the...
I sank down in a\the...
I sank down into my...
I sank down into the...
I sank down on a\the...
I sank down on my...
I sank down onto a\the...
I sank down onto my...
I sank down with a...

sat *verb*

I sat a\the...
I sat my...
I sat across a\the...
I sat across the...
I sat against the...
I sat among the...
I sat around a\the...
I sat as the...
I sat astride my...
I sat at a\an\the...
I sat at my...

I sat atop an...
I sat before the...
I sat behind my...
I sat behind the...
I sat beneath the...
I sat beside a\the...
I sat between my...
I sat between the...
I sat by a\the...
I sat by my...
I sat down a...
I sat for a\the...
I sat in a\an\the...
I sat in my...
I sat inside my...
I sat like a\an...
I sat near a\the...
I sat on a\the...
I sat on my...
I sat through the...
I sat under a\an\the...
I sat until my...
I sat until the...
I sat up a...
I sat upon a\the...
I sat upon my...
I sat with a\the...
I sat with my...
I sat within the...
I sat across from my...
I sat across from the...
I sat down across the...
I sat down against the...
I sat down at my...
I sat down at the...
I sat down behind a\the...
I sat down behind my...
I sat down beside my...
I sat down between a...
I sat down by the...
I sat down for a...
I sat down in a\the...

I sat down in my...
I sat down on a\an\the...
I sat down on my...
I sat down opposite the...
I sat down so my...
I sat down under a\the...
I sat down with a\the...
I sat down with my...
I sat nearest to the...
I sat out in my...
I sat out on the...
I sat up against the...
I sat up among the...
I sat up as the...
I sat up at the...
I sat up by the...
I sat up in my...
I sat up in the...
I sat up into the...
I sat up on my...
I sat up on the...
I sat up with a...

satisfaction *noun*

Satisfaction brimmed in...
Satisfaction burned in...
Satisfaction glinted in...
Satisfaction simmered in...

satisfied *verb*

I satisfied my...

sauntered *verb*

I sauntered from the...
I sauntered out the...
I sauntered to the...
I sauntered up the...
I sauntered out to the...
I sauntered over to the...
I sauntered up to the...

saved *verb*

I saved a\an\the...
I saved my...
I saved over the...
I saved up the...

savored *verb*

I savored my...
I savored the...

saw *verb*

I saw a\an\the...
I saw my...
I saw about a\the...
I saw against my...
I saw around the...
I saw as the...
I saw at a\the...
I saw before my...
I saw by the...
I saw during the...
I saw for the...
I saw from my...
I saw from the...
I saw in a\the...
I saw in my...
I saw of the...
I saw on my...
I saw on the...
I saw outside the...
I saw past the...
I saw through a\the...
I saw through my...
I saw to the...
I saw with a...
I saw with my...
I saw down in the...

sawed *verb*

I sawed my...
I sawed on my...

I sawed through the...

scaled *verb*
I scaled the...
I scaled down the...

scampered *verb*
I scampered down the...
I scampered like a...
I scampered out of the...

scanned *verb*
I scanned a\the...
I scanned my...
I scanned down the...
I scanned for a\the...
I scanned in the...
I scanned past the...
I scanned through the...

scar *noun*
Scars peeked out of...
A scar skidded down from...
The scar stood out in...
The scar stood out on...

scared *verb*
I scared the...
I scared of the...

scattered *verb*
I scattered the...
I scattered for an...
I scattered throughout the...

scene *noun*
The scene played out in...

scent *noun*
My scent drifted through...

The scent trailed off at...

scented *verb*
I scented the...

scheduled *verb*
I scheduled a...

school *noun*
The school cracked down on...

schooled *verb*
I schooled my...

scoffed *verb*
I scoffed a...
I scoffed at my...
I scoffed at the...
I scoffed under my...

scolded *verb*
I scolded the...

scooped *verb*
I scooped a\the...
I scooped my...
I scooped out a\the...
I scooped up a\the...
I scooped up my...

scooted *verb*
I scooted a\the...
I scooted my...
I scooted across the...
I scooted around the...
I scooted aside a...
I scooted down the...
I scooted into the...
I scooted onto the...
I scooted to the...

I scooted off through the...
I scooted off to my...
I scooted off to the...
I scooted out of the...
I scooted out to the...
I scooted up on my...

scored *verb*

I scored a\the...
I scored on my...
I scored on the...

scorned *verb*

I scorned the...

scoured *verb*

I scoured my...
I scoured the...
I scoured under the...

scouted *verb*

I scouted the...
I scouted out an...

scowl *noun*

My scowl deepened along with...

scowled *verb*

I scowled a...
I scowled at my...
I scowled at the...
I scowled for a\the...
I scowled into the...
I scowled toward the...
I scowled down at the...
I scowled up into the...

scrabbled *verb*

I scrabbled across the...
I scrabbled at the...

I scrabbled for the...
I scrabbled in my...
I scrabbled in the...
I scrabbled on the...
I scrabbled over the...
I scrabbled with my...
I scrabbled around in my...
I scrabbled around in the...
I scrabbled around on my...
I scrabbled around on the...
I scrabbled around through the...

scrambled *verb*

I scrambled a\the...
I scrambled across the...
I scrambled after the...
I scrambled around the...
I scrambled as the...
I scrambled behind the...
I scrambled down the...
I scrambled for a\an\the...
I scrambled for my...
I scrambled from the...
I scrambled into a\the...
I scrambled into my...
I scrambled off the...
I scrambled onto the...
I scrambled over a\the...
I scrambled though the...
I scrambled to a\an\the...
I scrambled to my...
I scrambled toward the...
I scrambled towards the...
I scrambled up the...
I scrambled down into the...
I scrambled down off the...
I scrambled out of my...
I scrambled out of the...
I scrambled over to the...
I scrambled up into the...
I scrambled up off the...

I scrambled up onto the...
I scrambled up to a...

scraped *verb*

I scraped a\the...
I scraped my...
I scraped against a...
I scraped at a...
I scraped at my...
I scraped up a\the...

scratched *verb*

I scratched my...
I scratched the...
I scratched at a\an\the...
I scratched at my...
I scratched behind my...
I scratched in the...
I scratched under my...
I scratched up a...
I scratched up my...

scrawled *verb*

I scrawled my...
I scrawled the...
I scrawled on my...

scream *noun*

Screams carried into...
Screams erupted from...
Screams rose as...
Screams sounded from...
A scream rose above
A scream tore from
A\the scream came from...
My scream broke through...
Screams shot up from...
The scream died with
The scream shrieked around
The scream went on
A scream tore out of...

My scream echoed off of...
My scream rang out like...
The scream cut off as...
The scream ripped out of...

screamed *verb*

I screamed a\an\the...
I screamed my...
I screamed against the...
I screamed around the...
I screamed as an\the...
I screamed as my...
I screamed at the...
I screamed for my...
I screamed into the...
I screamed like a...
I screamed on the...
I screamed out an\the...
I screamed through the...
I screamed to the...
I screamed until my...
I screamed with the...

screeched *verb*

I screeched my...
I screeched past the...
I screeched to a...

screen *noun*

A screen lit up inside...
The screen cut out before...
The screen flashed up that...
The screen lit up on...

screwed *verb*

I screwed my...
I screwed the...
I screwed on the...
I screwed up my...
I screwed up the...

scribbled *verb*

I scribbled a...
I scribbled my...
I scribbled down my...
I scribbled down the...
I scribbled in a\the...
I scribbled in my...
I scribbled on a\the...
I scribbled on my...
I scribbled out the...

scrolled *verb*

I scrolled a\the...
I scrolled down the...
I scrolled through my...
I scrolled through the...
I scrolled to a\the...
I scrolled through to the...

scrubbed *verb*

I scrubbed a\the...
I scrubbed my...
I scrubbed at my...
I scrubbed at the...
I scrubbed between my...
I scrubbed until my...

scrunched *verb*

I scrunched my...
I scrunched the...
I scrunched up my...

scrutinized *verb*

I scrutinized my...
I scrutinized the...

scuffed *verb*

I scuffed a\the...
I scuffed my...
I scuffed at the...

scurried *verb*

I scurried across the...
I scurried after the...
I scurried along a...
I scurried around the...
I scurried from the...
I scurried into the...
I scurried through the...
I scurried to a\the...
I scurried across to the...
I scurried off into a...
I scurried over to my...
I scurried over to the...

scuttled *verb*

I scuttled across the...
I scuttled along the...
I scuttled to my...
I scuttled over to a...

sealed *verb*

I sealed my...
I sealed the...

searched *verb*

I searched a\an\the...
I searched my...
I searched for a\an\the...
I searched for my...
I searched in the...
I searched through my...
I searched through the...

second *noun*

The second fell out of...

secured *verb*

I secured a\the...
I secured my...

seduced *verb*

I seduced a...

seemed *verb*

I seemed a\the...
I seemed at a...
I seemed in a...
I seemed like a\an\the...
I seemed of a...
I seemed on the...

seethed *verb*

I seethed for a...

seized *verb*

I seized a\an\the...
I seized my...
I seized on the...

selected *verb*

I selected a\an\the...
I selected my...

self-pity *noun*

Self-pity washed through...

self-preservation *noun*

Self-preservation kicked in...

sensation *noun*

Sensation tingled at...
Sensations boiled in...

sense *noun*

My senses seemed at...

sensed *verb*

I sensed a\the...
I sensed my...

sent *verb*

I sent a\an\the...
I sent my...
I sent away the...
I sent down a...
I sent for the...
I sent in a\the...
I sent in my...
I sent off a\an...
I sent off my...
I sent out a\an\the...
I sent out my...
I sent over the...
I sent to the...
I sent up a\the...

separated *verb*

I separated a\the...
I separated my...
I separated as a...
I separated out the...

served *verb*

I served a\the...
I served my...
I served as a\the...
I served for a...
I served in the...

set *verb*

I set a\an\the...
I set my...
I set about my...
I set aside my...
I set aside the...
I set down a\the...
I set down my...
I set for my...
I set in the...
I set off the...

I set out a...
I set out my...
I set to the...
I set up a\an\the...
I set up my...
I set off across the...
I set off at a\an...
I set off down the...
I set off for the...
I set off in the...
I set off into the...
I set off toward my...
I set off toward the...
I set off towards a\the...
I set off up the...
I set off without my...
I set out along the...
I set out down the...
I set out from my...
I set out in a...
I set out into the...
I set out on the...
I set up under my...

settled *verb*

I settled a\the...
I settled my...
I settled against a\the...
I settled at a\the...
I settled behind the...
I settled by the...
I settled for a\the...
I settled in the...
I settled into a\an\the...
I settled into my...
I settled like a...
I settled on a\the...
I settled on my...
I settled onto a\the...
I settled to my...
I settled with a...

I settled down against the...
I settled down in my...
I settled down on a...
I settled down with a...
I settled in to the...

severed *verb*

I severed my...
I severed the...

sex *noun*

My sex thrust up between...
My sex thrust up in...

shade *noun*

The shade rose out of...

shaded *verb*

I shaded my...
I shaded the...

shadow *noun*

Shadows advanced from...
Shadows closed about...
Shadows crawled across...
Shadows drifted at...
Shadows flickered across...
Shadows fought through...
Shadows hung about...
Shadows hung from...
Shadows leapt across...
Shadows moved at...
Shadows moved on...
Shadows played over...
Shadows raced across...
Shadows rolled across...
Shadows swung as...
Shadows took on...
A shadow appeared at
A shadow appeared on
A shadow fell across

A shadow fell from
A shadow fell on
A shadow fell over
A shadow flickered across
A shadow stood in
A shadow stood over
A\the shadow emerged from...
A\the shadow moved across...
A\the shadow moved in...
My shadow disappeared from...
My shadow fell over...
My shadow ran beside...
My shadow remained behind...
My shadow wavered on...
Shadows cast down by...
Shadows crept out of...
Shadows fell down from...
Shadows spun out of...
The shadow began as
The shadow flew through
The shadow stood behind
The shadow stood for
A shadow loomed out of...
A shadow stepped out from...
My shadow trailed out behind...
The shadow cast down by...
The shadow ducked down as...

shame *noun*

Shame burned within...
Shame followed on...
Shame slid through...
Shame swept through...
Shame washed over...
Shame washed through...

shared *verb*

I shared a\an\the...
I shared my...
I shared out the...
I shared with a...

I shared with my...

sharpened *verb*

I sharpened the...

shattered *verb*

I shattered a...
I shattered against the...
I shattered beneath the...

shaved *verb*

I shaved my...
I shaved off my...

sheathed *verb*

I sheathed my...
I sheathed the...

shed *verb*

I shed a\the...
I shed my...

sheet *noun*

A sheet pulled up over...

sheltered *verb*

I sheltered from a...
I sheltered in a...

shielded *verb*

I shielded my...

shifted *verb*

I shifted a\the...
I shifted my...
I shifted in my...
I shifted in the...
I shifted into a...
I shifted off the...
I shifted on my...

I shifted on the...
I shifted onto my...
I shifted so my...
I shifted to a\the...
I shifted up in my...

shimmered *verb*

I shimmered in the...

shimmied *verb*

I shimmied my...
I shimmied to the...
I shimmied out of my...
I shimmied out of the...

shined *verb*

I shined my...
I shined the...

ship *noun*

The ships left out in...

shipped *verb*

I shipped my...
I shipped the...

shirt *noun*

My shirt tore as...

shit *verb*

I shit my...
I shit in the...
I shit on the...

shivered *verb*

I shivered a\the...
I shivered against the...
I shivered as the...
I shivered at the...
I shivered because the...

I shivered despite the...
I shivered for a...
I shivered from the...
I shivered in my...
I shivered in the...
I shivered inside the...
I shivered like a...
I shivered under the...
I shivered with a\the...

shock *noun*

Shock crept over...
Shock flooded through...
Shock passed like...
Shock registered in...
Shock registered on...
Shock rippled through...
Shock splintered with...
Shock swept over...
Shock took that...
Shock turned into...

shone *verb*

I shone my...
I shone the...
I shone in the...
I shone with a...

shooed *verb*

I shooed the...
I shooed away the...

shook *verb*

I shook a\an\the...
I shook my...
I shook as the...
I shook away the...
I shook down the...
I shook from a...
I shook like a...
I shook off a\the...

I shook off my...
I shook out a\the...
I shook out my...
I shook with a\the...
I shook out of my...

shopped *verb*

I shopped a...
I shopped at my...
I shopped at the...

shot *noun*

Shots came from...
Shots poured through...
Shots rang out...
Shots rang out from...
A shot rang out against...
A shot rang out on...

shot *verb*

I shot a\an\the...
I shot my...
I shot at a\the...
I shot in the...
I shot into my...
I shot into the...
I shot like a...
I shot off a\the...
I shot out a\the...
I shot over my...
I shot through the...
I shot to my...
I shot up a...
I shot out of my...
I shot out of the...
I shot up from the...
I shot up off the...

shoulder *noun*

My shoulder crashed into...
My shoulder felt like...

My shoulder slammed into...
My shoulders eased as...
My shoulders felt like...
My shoulders sagged in...
My shoulders sagged with...
My shoulders shook as...
My shoulders shook with...
My shoulder bumped up against...
My shoulder butted up against...
My shoulders bunched up with...

shouldered *verb*

I shouldered a\the...
I shouldered my...
I shouldered between the...
I shouldered past a...
I shouldered through the...

shout *noun*

Shouts came from...
Shouts carried on...
Shouts rose around...
Shouts rose from...
Shouts sounded from...
Shouts rang out above...
A shout rang out from...
A shout rang up from...
A shout went up from...
A shout went up on...

shouted *verb*

I shouted a\an\the...
I shouted my...
I shouted as my...
I shouted as the...
I shouted at the...
I shouted down the...
I shouted for a\the...
I shouted for my...
I shouted from the...
I shouted in a\the...

I shouted into my...
I shouted into the...
I shouted out the...
I shouted over my...
I shouted over the...
I shouted to a\the...
I shouted to my...
I shouted toward the...
I shouted with the...

shoved *verb*

I shoved a\an\the...
I shoved my...
I shoved aside my...
I shoved aside the...
I shoved at my...
I shoved at the...
I shoved away the...
I shoved in a...
I shoved into an...
I shoved into my...
I shoved off the...
I shoved open my...
I shoved open the...
I shoved out a...
I shoved through the...
I shoved to my...
I shoved out of the...
I shoved up onto my...
I shoved up to my...

shoveled *verb*

I shoveled the...

showed *verb*

I showed a\the...
I showed my...
I showed off the...
I showed to the...
I showed up a...
I showed up at the...

I showed up for my...
I showed up for the...
I showed up in the...
I showed up with a...
I showed up with my...

showered *verb*

I showered for a...
I showered in my...
I showered in the...
I showered off the...

shrank *verb*

I shrank against the...
I shrank behind the...
I shrank from the...
I shrank into my...
I shrank down against the...

shredded *verb*

I shredded the...

shriek *noun*

A shriek went up like...

shrieked *verb*

I shrieked the...
I shrieked as the...
I shrieked behind my...

shriveled *verb*

I shriveled into my...

shrugged *verb*

I shrugged a\the...
I shrugged my...
I shrugged against the...
I shrugged at the...
I shrugged away the...
I shrugged into a\the...

I shrugged into my...
I shrugged like a...
I shrugged off my...
I shrugged off the...
I shrugged on a...
I shrugged with a...
I shrugged out of my...
I shrugged out of the...

shucked *verb*

I shucked a\the...
I shucked my...
I shucked off my...
I shucked off the...
I shucked out of my...

shudder *noun*

Shudders raced through...
A shudder rippled up from...

shuddered *verb*

I shuddered a...
I shuddered as an\the...
I shuddered at the...
I shuddered from the...
I shuddered with my...
I shuddered with the...

shuffled *verb*

I shuffled my...
I shuffled the...
I shuffled across the...
I shuffled along the...
I shuffled beside my...
I shuffled down the...
I shuffled inside the...
I shuffled into my...
I shuffled into the...
I shuffled like the...
I shuffled off the...
I shuffled through my...

I shuffled through the...
I shuffled to the...
I shuffled along with the...
I shuffled around in a...
I shuffled out into the...
I shuffled out of the...
I shuffled over in the...
I shuffled over to the...
I shuffled up from the...

shunned *verb*

I shunned the...

shut *verb*

I shut my...
I shut the...
I shut away the...
I shut down my...
I shut down the...
I shut off my...
I shut off the...
I shut out the...
I shut up in the...

shyness *noun*

Shyness gathered around...

side *noun*

My sides shook with...

sidestepped *verb*

I sidestepped a\the...
I sidestepped around a...
I sidestepped as a...
I sidestepped down the...
I sidestepped in the...

sidled *verb*

I sidled a...
I sidled around the...

I sidled to my...
I sidled up to the...

sifted *verb*

I sifted my...
I sifted through a\the...
I sifted through my...

sigh *noun*

A sigh stirred through
A sigh popped out before...
My sigh came out as...

sighed *verb*

I sighed a...
I sighed as my...
I sighed as the...
I sighed at the...
I sighed in my...
I sighed into the...
I sighed like a...
I sighed while my...
I sighed with the...
I sighed out through my...

sighted *verb*

I sighted the...
I sighted down my...

signaled *verb*

I signaled my...
I signaled the...
I signaled for my...
I signaled for the...
I signaled into the...
I signaled to a\the...
I signaled to my...

signed *verb*

I signed a\an\the...

I signed my...
I signed to a...
I signed with a\the...
I signed off with my...
I signed out of my...
I signed up for the...

silence *noun*

Silence crept around...
Silence crept over...
Silence crystallized about...
Silence descended like...
Silence descended on...
Silence descended over...
Silence descended upon...
Silence dragged on...
Silence echoed in...
Silence fell across...
Silence fell around...
Silence fell as...
Silence fell between...
Silence fell in...
Silence fell like...
Silence fell over...
Silence flowed in...
Silence followed by...
Silence greeted that...
Silence held for...
Silence hung between...
Silence hung in...
Silence hung on...
Silence hung over...
Silence lay over...
Silence lengthened while...
Silence lingered behind...
Silence poured in...
Silence presided over...
Silence rang through...
Silence reigned for...
Silence reigned in...
Silence seemed like...

Silence settled into...
Silence settled over...
Silence stole into...
Silence stretched on...
Silence whooshed in...
A silence dropped over
A silence fell across
A silence fell among
A silence fell between
A silence fell in
A silence fell over
A silence grew between
My silence went on...
Silence rippled out from...
Silence stretched out between...
The silence deepened around
The silence fell like
The silence felt like
The silence grew as
The silence lasted for
The silence persisted as
The silence rumbled like
The silence went on

silenced *verb*

I silenced my...
I silenced the...

singled *verb*

I singled out a\the...

sipped *verb*

I sipped a\the...
I sipped my...
I sipped at a\the...
I sipped at my...
I sipped for a...
I sipped from my...
I sipped from the...
I sipped on my...
I sipped through the...

I sipped until the...

siren *noun*

Sirens blared from...
Sirens sounded in...
Sirens cut out as...

sized *verb*

I sized up the...

skated *verb*

I skated the...
I skated down the...
I skated up to the...

sketched *verb*

I sketched a\an\the...
I sketched in a\the...
I sketched out the...
I sketched with the...

skidded *verb*

I skidded the...
I skidded across the...
I skidded against the...
I skidded around the...
I skidded into an...
I skidded on the...
I skidded to a...

skimmed *verb*

I skimmed a\the...
I skimmed my...
I skimmed over the...
I skimmed through a\the...
I skimmed through to the...

skin *noun*

My skin crawled at...
My skin crawled with...

My skin erupted in...
My skin felt like...
My skin looked like...
My skin sang with...
My skin shrank in...
My skin smelled of...
My skin tightened in...

skinned *verb*

I skinned my...
I skinned the...

skipped *verb*

I skipped a\an\the...
I skipped my...
I skipped across the...
I skipped off the...
I skipped through the...
I skipped to the...
I skipped out on the...
I skipped over to the...

skirted *verb*

I skirted a\the...
I skirted around the...
I skirted down a...

skittered *verb*

I skittered a...
I skittered around the...
I skittered over the...
I skittered over to the...

skull *noun*

My skull felt like...
My skull landed with...
My skull opened in...
My skull screamed as...

sky *noun*

The sky opened up above...
The sky opened up with...

slammed *verb*

I slammed a\the...
I slammed my...
I slammed against my...
I slammed against the...
I slammed down the...
I slammed in a\the...
I slammed into a\the...
I slammed on my...
I slammed on the...
I slammed to my...
I slammed to the...

slanted *verb*

I slanted a\the...
I slanted my...
I slanted to the...

slapped *verb*

I slapped a\an\the...
I slapped my...
I slapped at my...
I slapped at the...
I slapped away the...
I slapped open a\the...

slashed *verb*

I slashed a\the...
I slashed my...
I slashed at a\the...
I slashed open the...
I slashed through a\the...
I slashed out at the...
I slashed out with the...

sleep *noun*

Sleep came at...
Sleep came in...

Sleep came upon...
Sleep swept through...

slept *verb*

I slept a\the...
I slept my...
I slept as my...
I slept at the...
I slept atop the...
I slept beneath a...
I slept by the...
I slept for a\an...
I slept in a\the...
I slept in my...
I slept like a\the...
I slept on a\the...
I slept on my...
I slept through my...
I slept through the...
I slept under a...
I slept with a\the...
I slept with my...
I slept out on the...

slew *verb*

I slew my...
I slew the...

sliced *verb*

I sliced a\the...
I sliced my...
I sliced along the...
I sliced into my...
I sliced into the...
I sliced through the...
I sliced down at the...

slicked *verb*

I slicked my...

slid *verb*

I slid a\an\the...
I slid my...
I slid across a\the...
I slid against the...
I slid along the...
I slid behind the...
I slid between the...
I slid down my...
I slid down the...
I slid for a...
I slid from the...
I slid in a\an\the...
I slid into a\an\the...
I slid into my...
I slid off my...
I slid off the...
I slid on a\the...
I slid on my...
I slid onto a\the...
I slid open a\the...
I slid out a\an\the...
I slid out my...
I slid through the...
I slid to a\the...
I slid to my...
I slid under a\the...
I slid down along the...
I slid down from the...
I slid down in the...
I slid down into the...
I slid down onto my...
I slid down onto the...
I slid off of my...
I slid out from my...
I slid out of my...
I slid out of the...
I slid out onto the...
I slid over in the...
I slid up to a...

slipped *verb*

I slipped a\an\the...
I slipped my...
I slipped across the...
I slipped along the...
I slipped around the...
I slipped away the...
I slipped behind the...
I slipped below the...
I slipped between the...
I slipped down the...
I slipped from my...
I slipped from the...
I slipped in a\the...
I slipped inside the...
I slipped into a\an\the...
I slipped into my...
I slipped like a...
I slipped off my...
I slipped off the...
I slipped on a\an\the...
I slipped on my...
I slipped open the...
I slipped out my...
I slipped out the...
I slipped over a\the...
I slipped past the...
I slipped through a\the...
I slipped down below the...
I slipped down from my...
I slipped down into the...
I slipped down through the...
I slipped off to my...
I slipped out into the...
I slipped out of my...
I slipped out of the...
I slipped out to the...
I slipped over to my...
I slipped over to the...

slit *verb*

I slit my...
I slit the...
I slit open the...

slithered *verb*

I slithered my...
I slithered into the...
I slithered over the...
I slithered through the...

slogged *verb*

I slogged my...
I slogged through my...
I slogged through the...

sloshed *verb*

I sloshed a...
I sloshed over the...

slouched *verb*

I slouched a...
I slouched my...
I slouched behind the...
I slouched in a\the...
I slouched on the...
I slouched over the...

slowed *verb*

I slowed a\the...
I slowed my...
I slowed after a...
I slowed as the...
I slowed at a\the...
I slowed before a...
I slowed down a...
I slowed in a\the...
I slowed in my...
I slowed on the...
I slowed past a...
I slowed to a...
I slowed until the...
I slowed down for a...

slugged *verb*

I slugged the...
I slugged down a\the...

sluiced *verb*

I sluiced the...

slumped *verb*

I slumped a...
I slumped against a\the...
I slumped as an...
I slumped at the...
I slumped in a\the...
I slumped in my...
I slumped into a\the...
I slumped into my...
I slumped on my...
I slumped on the...
I slumped onto the...
I slumped over my...
I slumped over the...
I slumped to the...
I slumped down against a...
I slumped down beside the...
I slumped down in an\the...
I slumped down on a\the...
I slumped down onto the...

slung *verb*

I slung a\an\the...
I slung my...
I slung across my...

slunk *verb*

I slunk in a...
I slunk into the...
I slunk out of the...

slurped *verb*

I slurped my...
I slurped down a...

slurred *verb*

I slurred a...

smacked *verb*

I smacked my...
I smacked the...
I smacked into the...

smashed *verb*

I smashed a\an\the...
I smashed my...
I smashed in my...
I smashed into the...
I smashed out my...
I smashed through an...

smeared *verb*

I smeared a\an\the...
I smeared my...

smelled *verb*

I smelled a\the...
I smelled my...
I smelled like a...
I smelled of the...

smelt *verb*

I smelt the...
I smelt like a...

smile *noun*

A smile appeared on
A smile broke across
A smile broke over
A smile came across
A smile came over
A smile flickered across

A smile flickered around
A smile flickered at
A smile flickered on
A smile grew on
A smile hovered over
A smile tugged at
A smile wavered on
A smile widened on
My smile broadened as...
My smile died in...
My smile died on...
My smile disappeared as...
My smile disappeared before...
My smile felt like...
My smile stayed on...
My smile tugged at...
My smile wavered as...
My smile widened as...
The smile bled from
The smile came at
The smile came through
The smile died on
The smile disappeared from
The smile dropped from
The smile fell from
The smile fled as
The smile froze on
The smile remained on
The smile slipped from
The smile stayed in
The smile stayed on
The smile suggested that
The smile went from
A smile broke out across...
A smile broke out on...
A smile shone out of...
The smile faded along with...
The smile leaked out of...

smiled *verb*

I smiled a\an\the...

I smiled my...
I smiled across the...
I smiled as a\the...
I smiled at a\the...
I smiled at my...
I smiled because my...
I smiled despite my...
I smiled despite the...
I smiled for a\the...
I smiled in a\an\the...
I smiled into my...
I smiled into the...
I smiled like a\the...
I smiled over a...
I smiled over my...
I smiled through my...
I smiled through the...
I smiled with a\the...
I smiled with my...
I smiled down at my...
I smiled down at the...
I smiled over at my...
I smiled up at my...
I smiled up at the...

smirked *verb*

I smirked a...
I smirked at my...
I smirked in the...
I smirked into my...
I smirked into the...
I smirked within my...

smoke *noun*

Smoke belched from...
Smoke billowed above...
Smoke billowed across...
Smoke billowed from...
Smoke boiled from...
Smoke curled around...
Smoke curled from...

Smoke drifted from...
Smoke drifted into...
Smoke drifted through...
Smoke effused from...
Smoke floated in...
Smoke hung in...
Smoke hung over...
Smoke issued from...
Smoke leaked from...
Smoke poured from...
Smoke poured into...
Smoke puffed from...
Smoke rose above...
Smoke rose from...
Smoke rose in...
Smoke rose toward...
Smoke spiraled from...
Smoke spiraled over...
Smoke stabbed at...
Smoke swirled around...
Smoke swirled from...
Smoke swirled in...
Smoke trailed from...
Smoke unfurled in...
Smoke curled up around...
Smoke curled up from...
Smoke drifted up from...
Smoke oozed out of...
Smoke ribboned up from...
Smoke rolled out of...
Smoke rose out of...
The smoke rose up through...

smoked *verb*

I smoked a\an...
I smoked my...
I smoked in the...
I smoked like a...

smoothed *verb*

I smoothed a\an\the...

I smoothed my...
I smoothed down my...
I smoothed down the...
I smoothed out my...
I smoothed out the...

smothered *verb*

I smothered the...

snake *noun*

Snakes slithered in...
The snake curled up on...
The snake slithered off in...

snaked *verb*

I snaked a\an...
I snaked my...
I snaked along the...
I snaked between the...
I snaked out an...

snapped *verb*

I snapped a\the...
I snapped my...
I snapped into the...
I snapped off a\the...
I snapped on my...
I snapped on the...
I snapped open my...
I snapped open the...
I snapped out a\the...
I snapped out of my...
I snapped out of the...

snared *verb*

I snared my...
I snared the...

snarl *noun*

A snarl curled up from...

A snarl rumbled out of...

snarled *verb*

I snarled a\the...
I snarled at the...
I snarled like a...
I snarled to the...
I snarled under my...
I snarled with the...

snatched *verb*

I snatched a\the...
I snatched my...
I snatched at the...
I snatched for the...
I snatched from my...
I snatched off my...
I snatched up a\the...
I snatched up my...

sneaked *verb*

I sneaked a...
I sneaked my...
I sneaked across the...
I sneaked along the...
I sneaked into a\the...
I sneaked off the...
I sneaked out the...
I sneaked to the...
I sneaked off to the...
I sneaked out of the...
I sneaked up on the...
I sneaked up to the...

sneakers *noun*

My sneakers slid on...

sneered *verb*

I sneered at the...

sneezed *verb*

I sneezed into the...

snickered *verb*

I snickered a...
I snickered in a...

sniffed *verb*

I sniffed a\the...
I sniffed my...
I sniffed as the...
I sniffed at my...
I sniffed at the...
I sniffed in the...
I sniffed up a...

sniggered *verb*

I sniggered at my...
I sniggered through the...

snipped *verb*

I snipped the...

snored *verb*

I snored with a...

snorted *verb*

I snorted a\an\the...
I snorted my...
I snorted at the...
I snorted out a...
I snorted through my...
I snorted under my...
I snorted with a...

snow *noun*

The snow came down in...
The snow came up over...
The snow melted off in...
The snow piled up in...

The snow swirled down around...

snowflake *noun*

Snowflakes fell around...
Snowflakes settled on...
Snowflakes fluttered down like...

snuck *verb*

I snuck a...
I snuck my...
I snuck around the...
I snuck in a...
I snuck into my...
I snuck into the...
I snuck out the...
I snuck to the...
I snuck up the...
I snuck out of my...
I snuck out of the...

snuffed *verb*

I snuffed my...
I snuffed the...

snuggled *verb*

I snuggled a\the...
I snuggled my...
I snuggled against the...
I snuggled between the...
I snuggled in the...
I snuggled into a\the...
I snuggled on the...
I snuggled under the...
I snuggled down in the...

soaked *verb*

I soaked a\the...
I soaked my...
I soaked in the...
I soaked under the...
I soaked up the...

soared *verb*

I soared above the...
I soared across the...

sob *noun*

Sobs came through...
Sobs rose from...
Sobs poured out of...
Sobs rose out of...
A sob choked out of...
A sob ripped out of...
The sobs came out of...
The sobs ripped out of...

sobbed *verb*

I sobbed a...
I sobbed behind my...
I sobbed for a...
I sobbed into my...
I sobbed into the...
I sobbed like a...
I sobbed through the...

sobered *verb*

I sobered up in a...

softened *verb*

I softened a\the...
I softened my...
I softened for the...

sold *verb*

I sold a\the...
I sold my...
I sold off my...

solved *verb*

I solved the...

soothed *verb*
I soothed the...

sorrow *noun*
Sorrow drifted down from...

sorted *verb*
I sorted the...
I sorted out the...
I sorted through the...

sought *verb*
I sought a\the...
I sought for an...
I sought out the...

soul *noun*
My soul eased as...
My soul lit up like...

sound *noun*
Sounds approached from...
Sounds came from...
Sounds rushed in...
Sounds thundered in...
Sounds darted out of...
Sounds drifted up on...
Sounds rose out of...
A sound curled up from...
A sound rose out of...
A\the sound came out of...
The sound came up through...

sounded *verb*
I sounded a\the...
I sounded like a\an\the...
I sounded like my...
I sounded on the...
I sounded out the...

spaced *verb*
I spaced out my...

spared *verb*
I spared a\the...

spark *noun*
Sparks appeared at...
Sparks cascaded across...
Sparks erupted as...
Sparks exploded from...
Sparks flashed like...
Sparks flew as...
Sparks flew from...
Sparks flew like...
Sparks flew with...
Sparks flickered over...
Sparks leapt into...
Sparks lit on...
Sparks went on...
Sparks flew up from...
Sparks shot out in...
Sparks spiraled up in...
A spark lashed out from...
The spark went out of...

sparked *verb*
I sparked a...

spasm *noun*
Spasms surged through...

spat *verb*
I spat a\the...
I spat at the...
I spat in my...
I spat into the...
I spat like a...
I spat on my...
I spat on the...

I spat out a\the...
I spat out my...
I spat over the...
I spat to the...
I spat on to the...

spear *noun*

Spears thrust at...

speared *verb*

I speared a\the...
I speared my...

specialized *verb*

I specialized in the...

speculation *noun*

Speculation swirled in...

sped *verb*

I sped the...
I sped across the...
I sped down the...
I sped for a...
I sped into the...
I sped over the...
I sped through a\the...
I sped to a\the...
I sped toward the...
I sped up my...
I sped off in the...
I sped out of the...
I sped up to a...

speed *noun*

Speed increased by...

spelled *verb*

I spelled my...
I spelled the...

I spelled out the...

spent *verb*

I spent a\an\the...
I spent my...
I spent as a...
I spent at the...
I spent in a\the...
I spent in my...
I spent on a...
I spent over a\an...
I spent with the...

spewed *verb*

I spewed about my...
I spewed out my...

spider *noun*

The spider jumped off of...

spied *verb*

I spied a\an\the...
I spied from the...
I spied on my...
I spied under my...

spiked *verb*

I spiked a...

spilled *verb*

I spilled a\the...
I spilled my...
I spilled onto the...

spine *noun*

My spine broke in...

spirit *noun*

My spirits rose at...

spit *noun*

Spit bubbled at...
Spit flew as...
Spit flew from...
Spit nosed through...
Spit ran from...
Spit splashed into...
Spit ran out of...

spit *verb*

I spit the...
I spit at the...
I spit in my...
I spit in the...
I spit into the...
I spit like a...
I spit on the...
I spit out a\the...
I spit over my...
I spit under my...

spittle *noun*

Spittle flew from...
Spittle foamed at...
Spittle gleamed on...
Spittle landed on...
Spittle oozed from...

splashed *verb*

I splashed a\the...
I splashed my...
I splashed across a...
I splashed in the
I splashed into the...
I splashed on the...
I splashed though the...
I splashed through a\the...
I splashed down in the...
I splashed out to my...

splayed *verb*

I splayed my...
I splayed the...

split *verb*

I split my...
I split the...

spluttered *verb*

I spluttered to a...

spoiled *verb*

I spoiled a...

spoke *verb*

I spoke a\the...
I spoke my...
I spoke about a\the...
I spoke against my...
I spoke around the...
I spoke at the...
I spoke for a\the...
I spoke from a\the...
I spoke from my...
I spoke in a\an\the...
I spoke in my...
I spoke into a\the...
I spoke into my...
I spoke like a...
I spoke near the...
I spoke of a\the...
I spoke of my...
I spoke on a\the...
I spoke over my...
I spoke over the...
I spoke through the...
I spoke to a\an\the...
I spoke to my...
I spoke with a\an\the...
I spoke with my...
I spoke along with the...

spooned *verb*

I spooned a...

sported *verb*

I sported an...

spotted *verb*

I spotted a\an\the...

I spotted my...

sprang *verb*

I sprang the...

I sprang at the...

I sprang down the...

I sprang from my...

I sprang from the...

I sprang into the...

I sprang on the...

I sprang onto a\the...

I sprang to my...

I sprang to the...

I sprang up the...

I sprang out of the...

I sprang up from my...

I sprang up onto the...

sprawled *verb*

I sprawled across the...

I sprawled in a\the...

I sprawled into the...

I sprawled off the...

I sprawled on my...

I sprawled on the...

I sprawled with my...

sprayed *verb*

I sprayed a\the...

I sprayed my...

spread *verb*

I spread a\the...

I spread my...

I spread across the...

I spread on the...

I spread out a\the...

I spread out my...

spring *noun*

Spring came in...

sprinkled *verb*

I sprinkled a...

sprinted *verb*

I sprinted the...

I sprinted across the...

I sprinted along the...

I sprinted around the...

I sprinted at my...

I sprinted behind the...

I sprinted down the...

I sprinted for the...

I sprinted out the...

I sprinted past a\the...

I sprinted through the...

I sprinted to my...

I sprinted to the...

I sprinted toward the...

I sprinted towards the...

I sprinted up the...

sprouted *verb*

I sprouted on the...

sprung *verb*

I sprung the...

I sprung off the...

spun *verb*

I spun a\the...

I spun my...
I spun at the...
I spun down the...
I spun in a\the...
I spun in my...
I spun like a...
I spun off the...
I spun on a...
I spun on my...
I spun past the...
I spun through a\the...
I spun to the...
I spun toward the...
I spun around in a...
I spun around in my...
I spun around near a...

spurred *verb*

I spurred my...

spurted *verb*

I spurted against the...

sputtered *verb*

I sputtered a...

squared *verb*

I squared my...
I squared up the...

squashed *verb*

I squashed my...

squatted *verb*

I squatted behind the...
I squatted beside the...
I squatted by the...
I squatted in an\the...
I squatted on the...
I squatted over the...

I squatted to the...
I squatted down beside the...
I squatted down on the...

squawked *verb*

I squawked until the...

squeaked *verb*

I squeaked a...

squealed *verb*

I squealed my...
I squealed as the...

squeezed *verb*

I squeezed a\the...
I squeezed my...
I squeezed around the...
I squeezed between the...
I squeezed inside a...
I squeezed into a...
I squeezed off a...
I squeezed onto the...
I squeezed open the...
I squeezed out a...
I squeezed out my...
I squeezed past the...
I squeezed through the...
I squeezed down on the...

squinted *verb*

I squinted a...
I squinted my...
I squinted against my...
I squinted against the...
I squinted around the...
I squinted as my...
I squinted as the...
I squinted at my...
I squinted at the...
I squinted down the...

I squinted in the...
I squinted into the...
I squinted out the...
I squinted past the...
I squinted through a\an\the...
I squinted down at the...
I squinted out at the...
I squinted up at the...
I squinted up from the...

squirmed *verb*

I squirmed a\the...
I squirmed in my...
I squirmed in the...
I squirmed on the...
I squirmed toward the...
I squirmed out into the...

stabbed *verb*

I stabbed a\the...
I stabbed my...
I stabbed at a\the...
I stabbed out my...
I stabbed with the...
I stabbed out with my...
I stabbed out with the...

stacked *verb*

I stacked my...
I stacked the...

staged *verb*

I staged a...
I staged my...

staggered *verb*

I staggered a...
I staggered across the...
I staggered after the...
I staggered against the...
I staggered around the...

I staggered as a...
I staggered at the...
I staggered down the...
I staggered from the...
I staggered in a...
I staggered into a\the...
I staggered like a...
I staggered off the...
I staggered on my...
I staggered onto the...
I staggered to a\the...
I staggered to my...
I staggered toward the...
I staggered under the...
I staggered up the...
I staggered with the...
I staggered off to my...
I staggered out along the...
I staggered out into the...
I staggered out of my...
I staggered out of the...
I staggered over to the...
I staggered up onto a...

stair *noun*

Stairs led down into...
The stairs spiraled down in...

staked *verb*

I staked out the...

stalked *verb*

I stalked my...
I stalked the...
I stalked across the...
I stalked around my...
I stalked down the...
I stalked into the...
I stalked over the...
I stalked through the...
I stalked to the...

I stalked toward the...
I stalked towards the...
I stalked up the...
I stalked along for a...
I stalked around to the...
I stalked off into the...
I stalked out of my...
I stalked out of the...
I stalked out without a...
I stalked over to my...
I stalked over to the...

stallion *noun*

My stallion leapt from...

stamina *noun*

My stamina dropped by...

stammered *verb*

I stammered a...
I stammered around a...
I stammered out an...

stamped *verb*

I stamped a\the...
I stamped my...
I stamped on the...
I stamped out my...
I stamped down on the...

star *noun*

Stars appeared in...
Stars exploded in...
Stars glittered above...
Stars hung over...
Stars poked through with...

stare *noun*

My stare fell upon...
My stare felt like...

stared *verb*

I stared a\the...
I stared my...
I stared across the...
I stared after the...
I stared around the...
I stared as the...
I stared at a\the...
I stared at my...
I stared between the...
I stared down the...
I stared for a...
I stared from a\the...
I stared in a\the...
I stared into a\the...
I stared into my...
I stared out the...
I stared over the...
I stared past the...
I stared through the...
I stared to the...
I stared toward the...
I stared until my...
I stared up the...
I stared across at the...
I stared around at the...
I stared down at a\the...
I stared down at my...
I stared down into my...
I stared down into the...
I stared down onto the...
I stared off across the...
I stared off in the...
I stared off into the...
I stared out across the...
I stared out at the...
I stared out beyond my...
I stared out into the...
I stared out of the...
I stared out over the...

I stared out through the...
I stared over at the...
I stared up at a\the...
I stared up at my...
I stared up into the...
I stared up through the...

starlight *noun*
Starlight shone down through...

started *verb*
I started a\an\the...
I started my...
I started across the...
I started after the...
I started along the...
I started around the...
I started as a...
I started at a\the...
I started at my...
I started away a...
I started below the...
I started down a\the...
I started for my...
I started for the...
I started from my...
I started from the...
I started in the...
I started off the...
I started on the...
I started out the...
I started to a...
I started to my...
I started toward a\the...
I started toward my...
I started up my...
I started up the...
I started with a\the...
I started with my...
I started down toward the...
I started off across the...

I started off as an...
I started off between the...
I started off up the...
I started off with an...
I started off without the...
I started out at a...
I started out of my...
I started out of the...
I started out with my...
I started out with the...
I started up toward the...

startled *verb*
I startled a\the...
I startled at my...
I startled at the...

stashed *verb*
I stashed my...
I stashed the...
I stashed away my...

stated *verb*
I stated the...
I stated for a...
I stated in the...
I stated down at my...

statement *noun*
The statement came across as...
The statement came out in...

stayed *verb*
I stayed a\the...
I stayed my...
I stayed about a...
I stayed above the...
I stayed as the...
I stayed at a\the...
I stayed away a...
I stayed behind the...

I stayed beside the...
I stayed by the...
I stayed for a\an...
I stayed in a\the...
I stayed in my...
I stayed near the...
I stayed on my...
I stayed on the...
I stayed to the...
I stayed under the...
I stayed until the...
I stayed with a\the...
I stayed with my...
I stayed within my...
I stayed out of the...
I stayed out on the...

steadied *verb*

I steadied my...
I steadied the...

steam *noun*

Steam billowed into...
Steam came from...
Steam curled around...
Steam drifted over...
Steam gushed from...
Steam gusted from...
Steam hung in...
Steam rolled from...
Steam rose from...
Steam slithered from...
Steam wafted over...
Steam boiled up from...

steeled *verb*

I steeled my...

steered *verb*

I steered the...
I steered down the...

I steered into the...
I steered off the...
I steered to the...
I steered around to the...

stench *noun*

A stench rose up from...

step *noun*

My steps faltered as...
The steps opened onto

stepped *verb*

I stepped a...
I stepped my...
I stepped across the...
I stepped around a\the...
I stepped around my...
I stepped around the...
I stepped behind the...
I stepped beneath the...
I stepped beyond the...
I stepped down the...
I stepped from my...
I stepped from the...
I stepped in a\the...
I stepped inside a\the...
I stepped inside my...
I stepped into a\an\the...
I stepped into my...
I stepped off my...
I stepped off the...
I stepped on a\the...
I stepped on my...
I stepped onto a\the...
I stepped onto my...
I stepped out the...
I stepped outside the...
I stepped over a\an\the...
I stepped past the...
I stepped through a\the...

I stepped to my...
I stepped to the...
I stepped toward my...
I stepped toward the...
I stepped towards the...
I stepped under the...
I stepped up my...
I stepped around to the...
I stepped away from the...
I stepped down from the...
I stepped down into a...
I stepped down off the...
I stepped down on the...
I stepped down onto the...
I stepped off into the...
I stepped off onto a...
I stepped off with my...
I stepped on to the...
I stepped out from the...
I stepped out into a\the...
I stepped out into my...
I stepped out of a\the...
I stepped out of my...
I stepped out on my...
I stepped out on the...
I stepped out onto a\the...
I stepped out through the...
I stepped out to the...
I stepped out with a...
I stepped over to a\the...
I stepped through into a...
I stepped through onto the...
I stepped up beside the...
I stepped up into the...
I stepped up on a\the...
I stepped up onto the...
I stepped up to my...
I stepped up to the...

stiffened *verb*

I stiffened a...

I stiffened my...
I stiffened against the...
I stiffened as the...
I stiffened at the...
I stiffened for a...
I stiffened in my...
I stiffened within the...

stifled *verb*

I stifled a\an\the...
I stifled my...

stilled *verb*

I stilled my...
I stilled the...
I stilled at the...
I stilled for a...

stillness *noun*

Stillness grew in...
Stillness spread out from...

stirred *verb*

I stirred a\the...
I stirred my...
I stirred at the...
I stirred in the...
I stirred on the...
I stirred with the...

stitched *verb*

I stitched my...
I stitched the...

stoked *verb*

I stoked the...

stole *verb*

I stole a\an\the...
I stole my...

I stole down a...
I stole from a\the...
I stole from my...
I stole over near the...

stomach *noun*

My stomach dropped as...
My stomach dropped in...
My stomach fell through...
My stomach felt like...
My stomach grumbled at...
My stomach hung over...
My stomach lurched as...
My stomach lurched at...
My stomach lurched with...
My stomach pitched with...
My stomach plummeted like...
My stomach rumbled as...
My stomach rumbled in...
My stomach rumbled with...
My stomach tightened as...
My stomach turned as...
My stomach dropped out from...
My stomach rolled over with...
My stomach seized up at...
My stomach turned over from...

stomped *verb*

I stomped a\the...
I stomped across the...
I stomped down the...
I stomped inside my...
I stomped into my...
I stomped into the...
I stomped off the...
I stomped on my...
I stomped on the...
I stomped out the...
I stomped to the...
I stomped toward the...
I stomped up the...

I stomped around behind my...
I stomped out of the...
I stomped out to the...
I stomped over to my...

stone *noun*

Stones fell about...
Stones tumbled from...

stood *verb*

I stood a\an\the...
I stood my...
I stood across the...
I stood against the...
I stood along the...
I stood among a\the...
I stood as the...
I stood astride the...
I stood at a\the...
I stood at my...
I stood atop the...
I stood before a\the...
I stood before my...
I stood behind a\the...
I stood behind my...
I stood below the...
I stood beneath a\an\the...
I stood beside a\the...
I stood between my...
I stood between the...
I stood by a\the...
I stood for a\the...
I stood from my...
I stood from the...
I stood in a\an\the...
I stood in my...
I stood inside a\the...
I stood like a\the...
I stood near the...
I stood off a...
I stood on a\an\the...

I stood on my...
I stood on the...
I stood outside an\the...
I stood over my...
I stood over the...
I stood through a...
I stood to the...
I stood under a\the...
I stood upon a\the...
I stood with a\an\the...
I stood with my...
I stood within a\an\the...
I stood across from the...
I stood around for a...
I stood aside as the...
I stood down by the...
I stood off to the...
I stood out like a...
I stood out on the...
I stood up after the...
I stood up behind the...
I stood up during the...
I stood up for a...
I stood up from my...
I stood up from the...
I stood up in my...
I stood up in the...
I stood up on a\the...
I stood up on my...
I stood up to my...
I stood up with a\the...

stooped *verb*

I stooped behind the...
I stooped for the...
I stooped in the...
I stooped over a\the...
I stooped to the...
I stooped under the...
I stooped down for a...

stopped *verb*

I stopped a\the...
I stopped my...
I stopped above my...
I stopped across the...
I stopped after a...
I stopped as a...
I stopped at a\an\the...
I stopped at my...
I stopped before a\an\the...
I stopped behind a...
I stopped beneath the...
I stopped beside a\the...
I stopped by a\an\the...
I stopped for a\the...
I stopped in a\the...
I stopped in my...
I stopped into a...
I stopped into my...
I stopped near a\the...
I stopped on a\the...
I stopped on my...
I stopped outside a\the...
I stopped outside my...
I stopped past a...
I stopped under the...
I stopped with a\the...
I stopped with my...
I stopped within a...
I stopped off at the...

stored *verb*

I stored my...
I stored the...

storm *noun*

Storm screamed in...
Storm wept with...
Storms came on...
The storm bore down upon...

stormed *verb*

I stormed the...
I stormed down the...
I stormed into the...
I stormed off into the...
I stormed out in a...
I stormed out of the...
I stormed over to the...

story *noun*

My story began with...

stowed *verb*

I stowed a\the...
I stowed my...

straddled *verb*

I straddled a\the...

straightened *verb*

I straightened a\the...
I straightened my...
I straightened between the...
I straightened from the...
I straightened in my...
I straightened in the...
I straightened on my...
I straightened out my...
I straightened to a...
I straightened up a...
I straightened with a\an...
I straightened up from my...
I straightened up from the...
I straightened up in the...
I straightened up on the...
I straightened up with a...

strained *verb*

I strained my...
I strained against my...

I strained against the...
I strained at my...
I strained at the...
I strained for a...
I strained with my...
I strained up on the...

strand *noun*

The strands floated out toward...

strangled *verb*

I strangled on my...

strapped *verb*

I strapped my...
I strapped the...
I strapped into the...
I strapped on my...

streaked *verb*

I streaked through the...
I streaked up the...

streamed *verb*

I streamed from the...

strength *noun*

Strength emanated from...
Strength surged through...
The strength flowed out of...
The strength ran out of...
The strength went out of...

strengthened *verb*

I strengthened my...

stressed *verb*

I stressed the...

stretched *verb*

I stretched a\the...
I stretched my...
I stretched beneath the...
I stretched from the...
I stretched in a\the...
I stretched like a...
I stretched out a...
I stretched out my...
I stretched with a...
I stretched out on my...
I stretched out on the...
I stretched out with a...
I stretched out with my...
I stretched up on my...

stride *noun*

My stride continued as...

stripped *verb*

I stripped my...
I stripped the...
I stripped away the...
I stripped off a\the...
I stripped off my...
I stripped outside my...
I stripped to my...
I stripped out of my...
I stripped out of the...

strode *verb*

I strode the...
I strode across the...
I strode around the...
I strode between my...
I strode between the...
I strode down the...
I strode from the...
I strode into a\the...
I strode on a...
I strode out the...
I strode past the...

I strode through a\the...
I strode through the...
I strode to the...
I strode toward my...
I strode toward the...
I strode up the...
I strode along in my...
I strode down into the...
I strode off to the...
I strode out of an\the...
I strode out of my...
I strode out onto the...
I strode over to a\the...
I strode over to my...
I strode up to the...

stroked *verb*

I stroked a\the...
I stroked my...

strolled *verb*

I strolled across the...
I strolled along the...
I strolled around the...
I strolled in the...
I strolled into the...
I strolled like a...
I strolled past the...
I strolled through the...
I strolled to a\the...
I strolled toward an\the...
I strolled up the...
I strolled around to the...
I strolled out into the...
I strolled out of the...
I strolled out to the...
I strolled over to my...

strove *verb*

I strove with the...

struck *verb*

I struck a\an\the...
I struck my...
I struck along the...
I struck at the...
I struck from the...
I struck in a...
I struck with a...
I struck with my...
I struck within the...
I struck down at the...
I struck off with a...
I struck out at the...
I struck out in the...
I struck out on my...
I struck out towards the...

struggled *verb*

I struggled a...
I struggled against my...
I struggled against the...
I struggled as the...
I struggled beneath the...
I struggled down the...
I struggled during the...
I struggled for a\the...
I struggled for my...
I struggled from my...
I struggled in a\the...
I struggled in my...
I struggled into my...
I struggled on the...
I struggled through my...
I struggled through the...
I struggled to a\the...
I struggled to my...
I struggled under the...
I struggled up a\the...
I struggled with a\the...
I struggled with my...
I struggled out of my...

I struggled up from the...
I struggled up through the...

strung *verb*

I strung my...
I strung the...

strutted *verb*

I strutted around the...
I strutted onto the...

stubbed *verb*

I stubbed my...
I stubbed out my...
I stubbed out the...

stuck *verb*

I stuck a\an\the...
I stuck my...
I stuck in my...
I stuck on my...
I stuck on the...
I stuck out a\the...
I stuck out my...
I stuck to my...
I stuck to the...
I stuck with my...
I stuck with the...
I stuck up in the...

studied *verb*

I studied a\an\the...
I studied my...
I studied around the...
I studied at the...
I studied under a...
I studied with my...

stuffed *verb*

I stuffed a\the...

I stuffed my...

stumbled *verb*

I stumbled a\the...
I stumbled my...
I stumbled across the...
I stumbled against the...
I stumbled along the...
I stumbled as the...
I stumbled at the...
I stumbled by the...
I stumbled down a\the...
I stumbled during a...
I stumbled from the...
I stumbled in my...
I stumbled in the...
I stumbled into a\the...
I stumbled into my...
I stumbled off the...
I stumbled on a\the...
I stumbled onto the...
I stumbled over a\the...
I stumbled through the...
I stumbled to a\the...
I stumbled to my...
I stumbled under the...
I stumbled up a\the...
I stumbled upon a...
I stumbled around with the...
I stumbled on to the...
I stumbled out across the...
I stumbled out of the...
I stumbled over to the...
I stumbled up through the...

stunned *verb*

I stunned the...

stuttered *verb*

I stuttered a\the...
I stuttered my...

I stuttered over the...
I stuttered through a...
I stuttered to a...

submerged *verb*

I submerged my...
I submerged the...

submitted *verb*

I submitted a\an...
I submitted under the...

subsided *verb*

I subsided against the...
I subsided onto the...
I subsided with an...

succumbed *verb*

I succumbed for a...

sucked *verb*

I sucked a\the...
I sucked my...
I sucked at a\the...
I sucked down a...
I sucked in a\the...
I sucked in my...
I sucked on an\the...
I sucked on my...
I sucked down until my...

suckled *verb*

I suckled at the...

sued *verb*

I sued the...

suffered *verb*

I suffered a...
I suffered for a...

I suffered from the...
I suffered in the...
I suffered through a...

suggested *verb*

I suggested a\an\the...
I suggested to my...

suited *verb*

I suited the...

summarized *verb*

I summarized my...
I summarized the...

summoned *verb*

I summoned a\the...
I summoned my...
I summoned up my...
I summoned up the...

sun *noun*

The sun beat down on...
The sun beat down with...
The sun crept down between...
The sun dipped down behind...
The sun jumped out from...
The sun sailed out from...
The sun scorched down with...
The sun shone down on...

sunk *verb*

I sunk my...
I sunk the...
I sunk into a...

sunlight *noun*

The sunlight seemed out of...

sunset *noun*

Sunset burned like...

supported *verb*

I supported my...
I supported the...

supposed *verb*

I supposed a\the...
I supposed my...
I supposed by my...
I supposed if the...
I supposed in a...
I supposed since the...

suppressed *verb*

I suppressed a\an\the...
I suppressed my...

surface *noun*

The surface bubbled out like...

surfaced *verb*

I surfaced a\the...
I surfaced from the...
I surfaced on the...
I surfaced with a...

surged *verb*

I surged a...
I surged across the...
I surged at the...
I surged into the...
I surged to my...
I surged toward the...

surprise *noun*

Surprise flashed in...
Surprise flickered in...
Surprise flickered over...
Surprise fluttered through...

Surprise reflected in...
Surprise registered on...
Surprise showed on...

surprised *verb*

I surprised a...

surrendered *verb*

I surrendered my...
I surrendered to the...

surrounded *verb*

I surrounded the...

surveyed *verb*

I surveyed my...
I surveyed the...

survived *verb*

I survived a\the...
I survived my...

suspected *verb*

I suspected a\the...
I suspected my...

suspicion *noun*

Suspicion flared in...
Suspicion hung over...
Suspicion sliced through...

swabbed *verb*

I swabbed the...

swallowed *verb*

I swallowed a\the...
I swallowed my...
I swallowed against a\the...
I swallowed against my...
I swallowed as my...

I swallowed at the...
I swallowed because the...
I swallowed down a\the...
I swallowed down my...
I swallowed on a\an...
I swallowed on my...
I swallowed past a\the...
I swallowed past my...
I swallowed up the...
I swallowed with a...

swam *verb*

I swam a...
I swam along the...
I swam beneath the...
I swam down the...
I swam for the...
I swam in a...
I swam past the...
I swam to the...
I swam toward the...
I swam towards the...
I swam under the...
I swam underneath the...
I swam with a...
I swam with my...
I swam down below the...
I swam off toward my...
I swam out into the...
I swam out of the...
I swam out to the...
I swam over to the...

swapped *verb*

I swapped a\the...
I swapped my...
I swapped at the...
I swapped out my...
I swapped through the...

swarmed *verb*

I swarmed across the...
I swarmed into a\the...
I swarmed up a...

swatted *verb*

I swatted a\the...

swayed *verb*

I swayed a...
I swayed my...
I swayed for a...
I swayed in the...
I swayed on my...
I swayed so my...
I swayed to the...
I swayed with the...

sweat *noun*

Sweat beaded on...
Sweat bloomed on...
Sweat bloomed over...
Sweat dribbled from...
Sweat dripped from...
Sweat flew in...
Sweat gathered on...
Sweat gleamed across...
Sweat gleamed in...
Sweat gleamed on...
Sweat glistened at...
Sweat glistened on...
Sweat glistened through...
Sweat poured from...
Sweat poured off...
Sweat poured through...
Sweat prickled like...
Sweat ran from...
Sweat ran in...
Sweat ran into...
Sweat ran like...
Sweat sizzled on...
Sweat slid between...

Sweat streamed from...
Sweat trickled between...
Sweat trickled from...
Sweat trickled under...
Sweat broke out across...
Sweat broke out on...
Sweat broke out over...
Sweat broke out under...
Sweat popped out in...
Sweat popped out on...
Sweat rolled down from...
Sweat stood out on...
Sweat trickled down between...
Sweat trickled down under...
The sweat broke out on...

sweated *verb*

I sweated through my...

swept *verb*

I swept a\an\the...
I swept my...
I swept along the...
I swept around a...
I swept aside my...
I swept aside the...
I swept away a...
I swept from the...
I swept in a...
I swept into the...
I swept off my...
I swept on my...
I swept out the...
I swept over the...
I swept past a\the...
I swept through a\the...
I swept through my...
I swept to the...
I swept up the...
I swept off toward the...
I swept out of the...

I swept up into the...
I swept up to the...

swerved *verb*

I swerved the...
I swerved between the...
I swerved into the...
I swerved through the...
I swerved to the...
I swerved aside like a...

swiped *verb*

I swiped a\the...
I swiped my...
I swiped at my...
I swiped at the...
I swiped into the...
I swiped open the...
I swiped with the...
I swiped over to the...

swirled *verb*

I swirled my...
I swirled the...
I swirled off my...

swished *verb*

I swished my...
I swished the...

switched *verb*

I switched my...
I switched the...
I switched off my...
I switched off the...
I switched on a\the...
I switched on my...
I switched out the...
I switched to my...
I switched to the...
I switched over to the...

swiveled *verb*

I swiveled my...
I swiveled the...
I swiveled in my...
I swiveled in the...
I swiveled on my...
I swiveled on the...
I swiveled around in my...
I swiveled around to my...

swooped *verb*

I swooped my...
I swooped down like a...
I swooped out over the...

sword *noun*

Swords cut at...
Swords hacked at...
Swords rang on...
A sword appeared from
My sword dropped from...
My sword fell from...
My sword fell in...
My sword slid from...
The sword dropped from
The sword fell from
The sword slid into
The sword slipped from
The sword wavered in
The sword went into
The sword went through
A sword skittered off of...
The sword lashed out in...
The sword remained out of...
The sword slid down into...

swore *verb*

I swore a\an\the...
I swore my...
I swore as the...

I swore at a\the...
I swore beneath my...
I swore in my...
I swore to a...
I swore under my...

swung *verb*

I swung a\an\the...
I swung my...
I swung against the...
I swung astride my...
I swung at a\the...
I swung beneath the...
I swung by my...
I swung by the...
I swung for the...
I swung in a...
I swung into the...
I swung off the...
I swung onto a\the...
I swung onto my...
I swung open the...
I swung past the...
I swung to the...
I swung with my...
I swung around in my...
I swung around in the...
I swung around on my...
I swung around with a...
I swung around with my...
I swung down from my...
I swung out into the...
I swung out of the...
I swung out over the...
I swung up onto the...

sympathy *noun*

Sympathy simmered in...

T

tacked *verb*

I tacked the...
I tacked across the...
I tacked on a\an\the...
I tacked up a...

tackled *verb*

I tackled the...

tagged *verb*

I tagged my...
I tagged the...

tailed *verb*

I tailed the...

talked *verb*

I talked a\the...
I talked about a\the...
I talked about my...
I talked for a\an\the...
I talked in a...
I talked into the...
I talked like a\the...
I talked of my...
I talked of the...
I talked on the...
I talked through a\the...
I talked to a\an\the...
I talked to my...
I talked until the...
I talked with my...
I talked with the...

tamped *verb*

I tamped the...
I tamped down my...
I tamped down the...

tangled *verb*

I tangled my...

taped *verb*

I taped a\the...

tapped *verb*

I tapped a\an\the...
I tapped my...
I tapped at my...
I tapped at the...
I tapped on a\an\the...
I tapped on my...
I tapped open my...
I tapped out an...
I tapped with my...

targeted *verb*

I targeted my...
I targeted the...

taste *noun*

My taste exploded on...

tasted *verb*

I tasted my...
I tasted the...
I tasted in my...
I tasted like a...

taught *verb*

I taught a\an\the...
I taught my...
I taught at the...
I taught with a...

taunted *verb*

I taunted the...

taxi *noun*

The taxi pulled out into...
The taxi pulled up at...

taxied *verb*

I taxied from the...
I taxied to the...

tear *noun*

Tears appeared in...
Tears brimmed at...
Tears brimmed in...
Tears came into...
Tears fell from...
Tears fell on...
Tears fell onto...
Tears froze on...
Tears gathered at...
Tears gathered in...
Tears leaked from...
Tears looked like...
Tears materialized in...
Tears ran from...
Tears rose in...
Tears rose inside...
Tears seeped into...
Tears shimmered in...
Tears slipped from...
Tears spilled onto...
Tears spilled over...
Tears sprang behind...
Tears sprang into...
Tears started in...
Tears stood in...
Tears streamed from...
Tears swam in...
Tears swam over...
My tears came in...

My tears fell onto...
My tears spilled over...
Tears jumped out of...
Tears leaked out of...
Tears poured out of...
Tears ran out of...
Tears rose up in...
Tears stood out in...
Tears streaked down through...
Tears welled up in...
The tears came at
The tears came in
The tears fell from
The tears started in
A tear slipped out from...
A tear slipped out of...
My tears ran down between...
The tears came down like...

teased *verb*

I teased a\the...
I teased out the...

teetered *verb*

I teetered a...
I teetered for a\an...
I teetered on the...

television *noun*

Televisions blared on...
A television blared out from...

temptation *noun*

Temptation nudged at...

tended *verb*

I tended the...
I tended to the...

tenderness *noun*

Tenderness blended with...
Tenderness shone in...
Tenderness swelled in...

tensed *verb*

I tensed a...
I tensed my...
I tensed against the...
I tensed as the...
I tensed at the...
I tensed despite the...
I tensed up a...

tension *noun*

Tension boomed between...
Tension crackled in...
Tension crackled through...
Tension eased from...
Tension knotted in...
Tension radiated from...
Tension seeped into...
Tension simmered through...
Tension snaked across...
Tension stretched across...
Tension unknotted inside...
Tension vibrated through...

terror *noun*

Terror blasted through...
Terror came with...
Terror clutched at...
Terror flashed over...
Terror flickered after...
Terror lanced through...
Terror leaped into...
Terror lurked at...
Terror rose in...
Terror shot through...
Terror wrapped around...
Terror flashed up in...
Terror rose up on...

tested *verb*

I tested a\the...
I tested my...
I tested in the...

testified *verb*

I testified the...
I testified about my...
I testified at the...
I testified before the...
I testified in the...

texted *verb*

I texted a...
I texted my...
I texted on a...

thanked *verb*

I thanked a\the...
I thanked my...

thigh *noun*

My thigh came between...

thing *noun*

The thing cried out in...

thirst *noun*

Thirst clawed at...
Thirst rolled up on...

thought *noun*

Thoughts came into...
Thoughts circled in...
Thoughts crashed through...
Thoughts poured like...
Thoughts raced through...
My thoughts drifted as...
My thoughts drifted from...

My thoughts drifted toward...
My thoughts meandered until...
My thoughts raced through...
My thoughts ran on...
My thoughts tumbled over...
Thoughts rattled around in...
My thoughts broke off as...
My thoughts broke off with...
My thoughts cleared up in...
The thought broke off as...

thought *verb*

I thought a\an\the...
I thought my...
I thought about a\an\the...
I thought about my...
I thought after a...
I thought as my...
I thought as the...
I thought at the...
I thought for a\an\the...
I thought from the...
I thought if the...
I thought in a\an\the...
I thought of a\an\the...
I thought of my...
I thought on my...
I thought through a...
I thought to my...
I thought to the...
I thought up the...
I thought with a\an\the...

thrashed *verb*

I thrashed my...
I thrashed against the...
I thrashed in the...
I thrashed inside the...
I thrashed on the...

threaded *verb*

I threaded my...
I threaded the...

threatened *verb*

I threatened the...

threw *verb*

I threw a\an\the...
I threw my...
I threw aside the...
I threw at the...
I threw away my...
I threw away the...
I threw down an\the...
I threw down my...
I threw in a\the...
I threw in my...
I threw like a...
I threw off my...
I threw off the...
I threw on a\the...
I threw on my...
I threw open my...
I threw open the...
I threw out a\the...
I threw out my...
I threw over my...
I threw up a\an\the...
I threw up my...
I threw up in my...
I threw up in the...
I threw up on my...
I threw up on the...

thrived *verb*

I thrived in the...

throat *noun*

My throat closed as...
My throat closed in...
My throat felt like...

My throat moved as...
My throat tightened against...
My throat tightened as...
My throat tightened until...
My throat tightened with...
My throat worked as...
My throat worked in...
My throat worked on...
My throat closed up as...

throttled *verb*

I throttled the...
I throttled down the...

thrust *verb*

I thrust a\an\the...
I thrust my...
I thrust aside the...
I thrust at my...
I thrust out a\the...
I thrust out my...
I thrust over a...
I thrust with my...

thudded *verb*

I thudded onto the...

thumb *noun*

My thumb rubbed over...
My thumb slid between...
My thumb slid into...
My thumb slid over...
My thumb trailed over...

thumbed *verb*

I thumbed a\the...
I thumbed my...
I thumbed away a...
I thumbed down the...
I thumbed off the...
I thumbed on my...

I thumbed open the...
I thumbed through the...
I thumbed to a\the...

thumped *verb*

I thumped a\the...
I thumped my...
I thumped across the...
I thumped onto the...
I thumped to the...

thunder *noun*

Thunder boomed from...
Thunder boomed like...
Thunder boomed over...
Thunder crackled in...
Thunder echoed in...
Thunder flashed in...
Thunder growled through...
Thunder rolled across...
Thunder rolled in...
Thunder rumbled as...
Thunder rumbled at...
Thunder rumbled from...
Thunder rumbled in...
Thunder sounded beneath...
Thunder thumped in...
Thunder rolled out of...

thundered *verb*

I thundered my...
I thundered across my...
I thundered down the...

ticked *verb*

I ticked off a\the...

tickled *verb*

I tickled my...
I tickled the...

tidied *verb*

I tidied the...
I tidied up the...

tied *verb*

I tied a\an\the...
I tied my...
I tied off the...
I tied on my...
I tied on the...
I tied to the...
I tied up my...

tightened *verb*

I tightened my...
I tightened the...
I tightened down on the...
I tightened up on my...

tilted *verb*

I tilted a\the...
I tilted my...
I tilted up my...

time *noun*

Time dragged on...
Time flew by...
Time froze for...
Time froze in...
Time marched on...
Time moved on...
Time passed in...
Time passed inside...
Time restarted with...
Time rushed over...
Time slowed as...
Time slowed at...
Time slowed for...
Time spent with...
Time stole from...
Time stopped as...

Time stretched on...
Time trudged by...
Time wore on...
Time worked against...

timed *verb*

I timed my...
I timed the...

tingle *noun*

Tingles raced across...
Tingles raced along...

tipped *verb*

I tipped a\an\the...
I tipped my...
I tipped down my...
I tipped over the...

tiptoed *verb*

I tiptoed a...
I tiptoed around a...
I tiptoed into the...
I tiptoed past the...
I tiptoed through the...
I tiptoed out of the...

tire *noun*

Tires crunched across...
Tires screeched as...
Tires screeched behind...
Tires shrieked as...

toasted *verb*

I toasted the...
I toasted with my...

toe *noun*

My toe went in...
My toes curled at...

My toes curled into...

toed *verb*

I toed a\the...
I toed off my...
I toed through a...

told *verb*

I told a\an\the...
I told my...
I told about the...
I told of a\the...

tone *noun*

My tone hinted at...
My tone took on...

tongue *noun*

Tongue hung in...
My tongue dipped into...
My tongue felt as...
My tongue felt like...
My tongue flashed over...
My tongue flickered over...
My tongue hung over...
My tongue lashed at...
My tongue moved over...
My tongue rubbed over...
My tongue slid along...
My tongue slid over...
My tongue slid past...
My tongue worked over...
My tongue blew out of...
My tongue lolled out between...
My tongue lolled out in...
My tongue poked out of...
My tongue rolled out of...
My tongue swiped out over...

took *verb*

I took a\an\the...

I took my...
I took apart my...
I took as a...
I took away the...
I took down a\the...
I took from a\the...
I took from my...
I took in a\the...
I took in my...
I took into the...
I took of the...
I took off my...
I took off the...
I took on a\the...
I took out a...
I took out a\an\the...
I took out my...
I took outside the...
I took over the...
I took to my...
I took to the...
I took up a\the...
I took up my...
I took off after the...
I took off at a...
I took off down the...
I took off for the...
I took off into the...
I took off like a...
I took off on my...
I took off over the...
I took off to the...

tooth *noun*

Teeth flew like...
Teeth glowed like...
Teeth snapped at...
My teeth clicked as...
My teeth sank into...

topped *verb*

I topped a\the…
I topped off my…
I topped off the…
I topped up the…

toppled *verb*

I toppled over the…
I toppled to the…
I toppled over in my…

torch *noun*

Torches carried by…
Torches flickered along…
Torches flickered atop…
Torches mounted on…
Torches rested in…
My torch lay beside…
The torches fanned out in…

torchlight *noun*

Torchlight fell across…
Torchlight flared behind…
Torchlight ran along…
Torchlight spilled through…

tore *verb*

I tore a\the…
I tore my…
I tore across the…
I tore at my…
I tore at the…
I tore away the…
I tore down a\the…
I tore into my…
I tore into the…
I tore off a\the…
I tore off my…
I tore open a\the…
I tore open my…
I tore out the…
I tore past the…

I tore though the…
I tore through the…
I tore up the…
I tore around in a…
I tore off in a…
I tore out of the…

tormented *verb*

I tormented my…

tornado *noun*

Tornadoes blew out of…

tossed *verb*

I tossed a\an\the…
I tossed my…
I tossed aside my…
I tossed aside the…
I tossed down a\the…
I tossed down my…
I tossed in a…
I tossed in my…
I tossed off my…
I tossed off the…
I tossed on my…
I tossed onto my…
I tossed out a\the…
I tossed over the…
I tossed up my…

tottered *verb*

I tottered a…
I tottered my…
I tottered to a\the…
I tottered toward the…
I tottered around in a…

touch *noun*

My touch moved on…
My touch traveled along…

touched *verb*

I touched a\the...
I touched my...
I touched off the...
I touched up my...
I touched with the...

toured *verb*

I toured the...

tousled *verb*

I tousled my...

towed *verb*

I towed the...

toweled *verb*

I toweled the...

tower *noun*

The tower came down before...
The tower went up with...

toyed *verb*

I toyed with a\the...
I toyed with my...

traced *verb*

I traced a\an\the...
I traced my...

tracked *verb*

I tracked a\the...
I tracked down a\the...
I tracked down my...
I tracked to the...

traded *verb*

I traded a\the...
I traded my...

traffic *noun*

Traffic hummed from...
Traffic inched along...
Traffic parted in...
Traffic raced by...
Traffic backed up on...
Traffic picked up on...
The traffic lightened up once...

trail *noun*

The trail ran out across...

trailed *verb*

I trailed a\an\the...
I trailed my...
I trailed after the...
I trailed along the...
I trailed around the...
I trailed behind a...
I trailed into the...
I trailed along at the...
I trailed off as a\the...
I trailed off as my...
I trailed off into a...
I trailed off with a...
I trailed out of the...
I trailed over to my...
I trailed over to the...

train *noun*

Train stopped in...
A train seemed like
My train pulled in...
A train streaked out from...
The train moved off at...
The train pulled out of...
The train snaked up towards...

trained *verb*

I trained my...

I trained the...
I trained at a...
I trained under a...
I trained with an\the...

tramped *verb*

I tramped a...
I tramped across the...
I tramped along the...
I tramped into the...

transferred *verb*

I transferred my...
I transferred the...
I transferred from the...
I transferred to the...

transformed *verb*

I transformed the...

transmitted *verb*

I transmitted my...

trapped *verb*

I trapped the...

traveled *verb*

I traveled a\the...
I traveled my...
I traveled as the...
I traveled in a...
I traveled in my...
I traveled through the...
I traveled throughout the...
I traveled to the...
I traveled with a\the...
I traveled out of the...

travelled *verb*

I travelled a...

I travelled on the...
I travelled with the...

traversed *verb*

I traversed the...

treasured *verb*

I treasured the...

treated *verb*

I treated my...
I treated the...

tree *noun*

Trees exploded within...
Trees grew inside...
Trees grew throughout...
Trees thrashed in...
The tree leaned out across...
The trees grew up on...

trekked *verb*

I trekked the...
I trekked through the...

trembled *verb*

I trembled a...
I trembled at the...
I trembled from the...
I trembled on the...
I trembled with a...

trenchcoat *noun*

My trenchcoat flew behind...

trepidation *noun*

My trepidation felt like...

tricked *verb*

I tricked the...

trickle *noun*

A trickle ran down onto...

trickled *verb*

I trickled the...

tried *verb*

I tried a\an\the...
I tried my...
I tried as my...
I tried for a\an\the...
I tried for my...
I tried from my...
I tried in the...
I tried on a...
I tried on my...
I tried out a...
I tried until the...
I tried out for the...

triggered *verb*

I triggered my...
I triggered the...
I triggered off a...

trilled *verb*

I trilled my...
I trilled the...

trimmed *verb*

I trimmed my...

tripped *verb*

I tripped the...
I tripped on a\the...
I tripped over a\the...
I tripped over my...

triumph *noun*

Triumph flashed in...
Triumph flooded through...
Triumph gleamed in...
Triumph glittered in...

trod *verb*

I trod on a...
I trod on my...

trotted *verb*

I trotted my...
I trotted after a...
I trotted along the...
I trotted by the...
I trotted down the...
I trotted through the...
I trotted to my...
I trotted to the...
I trotted towards my...
I trotted up the...
I trotted over to the...

trouble *noun*

The trouble rose up in...

truck *noun*

The truck came down off...

trudged *verb*

I trudged across the...
I trudged along a\the...
I trudged down the...
I trudged into the...
I trudged out the...
I trudged over the...
I trudged past the...
I trudged through the...
I trudged to the...
I trudged toward the...
I trudged towards the...
I trudged until the...

I trudged up the...
I trudged out into the...
I trudged out of the...
I trudged over to my...

trumpet *noun*

Trumpets sounded from...
Trumpets sounded on...

trumpeted *verb*

I trumpeted my...
I trumpeted the...

trundled *verb*

I trundled into the...
I trundled down into the...

trusted *verb*

I trusted my...
I trusted the...
I trusted with the...

truth *noun*

Truth lit up in...

tucked *verb*

I tucked a\the...
I tucked my...
I tucked away the...
I tucked in my...
I tucked in the...

tugged *verb*

I tugged a\an\the...
I tugged my...
I tugged at a\an\the...
I tugged at my...
I tugged down my...
I tugged down the...
I tugged off a...

I tugged off my...
I tugged on a\an\the...
I tugged on my...
I tugged open my...
I tugged out the...
I tugged up my...

tumbled *verb*

I tumbled down the...
I tumbled in a...
I tumbled into the...
I tumbled off the...
I tumbled onto the...
I tumbled over the...
I tumbled through the...
I tumbled to the...
I tumbled out over the...

tuned *verb*

I tuned a\the...
I tuned out the...
I tuned to the...
I tuned in to the...
I tuned out for the...

tunnel *noun*

A tunnel led down into...

tunneled *verb*

I tunneled my...

turned *verb*

I turned a\an\the...
I turned my...
I turned as a\the...
I turned at a\the...
I turned at my...
I turned away a...
I turned down a\the...
I turned down my...
I turned for the...

I turned from a\the...
I turned from my...
I turned in a\the...
I turned in my...
I turned into a\an\the...
I turned into my...
I turned like a...
I turned off my...
I turned off the...
I turned on a\the...
I turned on my...
I turned on the...
I turned onto a\an\the...
I turned onto my...
I turned out my...
I turned out the...
I turned over the...
I turned so my...
I turned through the...
I turned to a\the...
I turned to my...
I turned toward my...
I turned toward the...
I turned towards my...
I turned towards the...
I turned up my...
I turned up the...
I turned upon the...
I turned with a\an\the...
I turned with my...
I turned around at the...
I turned around for a...
I turned around in my...
I turned around in the...
I turned around to the...
I turned around with a\an...
I turned away from the...
I turned in to the...
I turned off onto the...
I turned out of the...
I turned over on my...
I turned over onto my...

I turned up at the...
I turned up for my...
I turned up with an...

twig *noun*

Twigs snapped as...
Twigs snapped under...

twilight *noun*

Twilight faded into...
Twilight frowned at...
Twilight seeped through...
Twilight settled in...

twined *verb*

I twined my...

twinkled *verb*

I twinkled my...

twirled *verb*

I twirled a\the...
I twirled my...
I twirled down the...
I twirled through the...

twisted *verb*

I twisted a\the...
I twisted my...
I twisted against the...
I twisted aside my...
I twisted at the...
I twisted in my...
I twisted in the...
I twisted off the...
I twisted on my...
I twisted on the...
I twisted onto my...
I twisted open a...
I twisted open my...

I twisted out the...
I twisted to my...
I twisted to the...
I twisted up onto my...

twitched *verb*

I twitched a\the...
I twitched my...
I twitched at the...
I twitched in the...

typed *verb*

I typed a\the...
I typed my...
I typed at the...
I typed in a\the...
I typed in my...
I typed into the...
I typed on my...
I typed out a...
I typed out my...

 U

unbuckled *verb*
I unbuckled my...
I unbuckled the...

unbuttoned *verb*
I unbuttoned my...

uncapped *verb*
I uncapped the...

uncertainty *noun*
Uncertainty flashed in...
Uncertainty quivered in...
Uncertainty reflected in...

unclenched *verb*
I unclenched my...

unclipped *verb*
I unclipped a\the...
I unclipped my...

uncoiled *verb*
I uncoiled a...
I uncoiled my...
I uncoiled from the...

unconsciousness *noun*
Unconsciousness loomed like...

uncorked *verb*
I uncorked my...
I uncorked the...

uncovered *verb*
I uncovered a\the...

uncurled *verb*
I uncurled my...

underestimated *verb*
I underestimated the...

underlined *verb*
I underlined my...
I underlined the...

underpants *noun*
My underpants lay beside...

understanding *noun*
Understanding came in...
Understanding came into...
Understanding dawned as...
Understanding dawned in...
Understanding dawned on...
Understanding flashed in...
Understanding flickered over...
Understanding flooded through...
Understanding washed over...

understood *verb*
I understood a\the...
I understood my...
I understood for the...
I understood from the...
I understood in a...
I understood on a...

underwent *verb*
I underwent an...

undid *verb*
I undid a\the...

I undid my...

undressed *verb*

I undressed in the...
I undressed to my...

unearthed *verb*

I unearthed a...
I unearthed my...

unease *noun*

Unease crawled over...
Unease flickered in...
Unease snaked through...

uneasiness *noun*

Uneasiness stole through...

unfastened *verb*

I unfastened a\the...
I unfastened my...

unfolded *verb*

I unfolded a\an\the...
I unfolded my...
I unfolded from my...
I unfolded from the...

unfurled *verb*

I unfurled my...

unhooked *verb*

I unhooked a\the...
I unhooked my...

unlatched *verb*

I unlatched the...

unleashed *verb*

I unleashed a\the...

I unleashed my...

unloaded *verb*

I unloaded my...
I unloaded the...
I unloaded on the...

unlocked *verb*

I unlocked a\the...
I unlocked my...

unpacked *verb*

I unpacked a\the...
I unpacked my...
I unpacked in my...

unplugged *verb*

I unplugged the...

unraveled *verb*

I unraveled a\the...

unreality *noun*

Unreality washed over...

unrolled *verb*

I unrolled a\the...
I unrolled my...

unscrewed *verb*

I unscrewed my...
I unscrewed the...

unsheathed *verb*

I unsheathed a\the...
I unsheathed my...

unslung *verb*

I unslung the...

unsnapped *verb*

I unsnapped my...
I unsnapped the...

untied *verb*

I untied a\the...
I untied my...

unwound *verb*

I unwound my...
I unwound the...
I unwound from my...

unwrapped *verb*

I unwrapped a\the...
I unwrapped my...

unzipped *verb*

I unzipped a\the...
I unzipped my...

upended *verb*

I upended a\the...
I upended my...

uploaded *verb*

I uploaded the...

upped *verb*

I upped my...
I upped the...

urged *verb*

I urged my...
I urged the...

urine *noun*

Urine puddled onto...
Urine reeked from...

used *verb*

I used a\an\the...
I used my...
I used as a...
I used during my...
I used for my...
I used on my...
I used on the...
I used up a\the...

ushered *verb*

I ushered my...

uttered *verb*

I uttered a\the...

V

vacuumed *verb*

I vacuumed the...
I vacuumed beneath the...

valley *noun*

The valley opened up into...

van *noun*

The van bumped along past...
The van drove off before...
The van puttered along at...

vanished *verb*

I vanished beneath a...
I vanished from my...
I vanished from the...
I vanished in a...
I vanished into a\the...
I vanished on the...
I vanished over the...
I vanished through an\the...
I vanished under the...
I vanished without a...

varied *verb*

I varied my...

vaulted *verb*

I vaulted a\the...
I vaulted off my...
I vaulted off the...
I vaulted onto the...
I vaulted over the...
I vaulted through the...
I vaulted to my...

I vaulted out of the...
I vaulted up onto a...
I vaulted up to a...

veered *verb*

I veered across the...
I veered off the...
I veered toward the...
I veered over to the...

vein *noun*

My veins responded before...
The veins glowed with
Veins stood out at...
Veins stood out in...
Veins stood out on...
My veins lit up as...
My veins lit up with...
The veins stood out along...
The veins stood out on...

vengeance *noun*

Vengeance clawed at...

venom *noun*

Venom blazed in...
Venom dripped from...
Venom dripped in...

vented *verb*

I vented about my...

ventured *verb*

I ventured a...
I ventured into the...
I ventured near the...
I ventured out in the...
I ventured out into the...
I ventured out onto the...

vertigo *noun*

Vertigo washed over...

viewed *verb*

I viewed my...
I viewed the...

vision *noun*

Visions swam in...
A vision slammed into
My vision blurred as...
My vision blurred at...
My vision swam as...
My vision swam with...
My vision took on...
The vision appeared in
The vision came on
The vision leapt into

visited *verb*

I visited a\an\the...
I visited my...
I visited as a...
I visited on a...
I visited with the...

visualized *verb*

I visualized a\the...
I visualized my...

voice *noun*

Voices called around...
Voices came from...
Voices rose from...
Voices rose in...
Voices shouted for...
Voices sounded from...
Voices sounded in...
Voices swelled in...
A voice came over

A voice screamed in
A voice sighed across
A voice spoke behind
A voice spoke beside
A voice spoke from
A\the voice came from...
A\the voice came on...
A\the voice spoke in...
My voice broke as...
My voice broke at...
My voice broke on...
My voice broke with...
My voice came as...
My voice came at...
My voice came from...
My voice came in...
My voice came like...
My voice climbed with...
My voice deepened without...
My voice died as...
My voice dropped at...
My voice dropped into...
My voice dropped on...
My voice dropped until...
My voice exploded into...
My voice faltered at...
My voice felt like...
My voice flowed over...
My voice got into...
My voice grabbed at...
My voice lowered as...
My voice lowered in...
My voice lowered until...
My voice lowered with...
My voice rang against...
My voice rang in...
My voice rang like...
My voice rang through...
My voice rang with...
My voice rose above...
My voice rose in...
My voice rose into...

My voice rose on...
My voice rose over...
My voice rose through...
My voice rose with...
My voice sank into...
My voice shook as...
My voice shook with...
My voice slid through...
My voice sounded like...
My voice spoke in...
My voice tightened in...
My voice took on...
My voice trailed into...
My voice wavered as...
My voice wavered toward...
My voice went on...
The voice sounded like
Voices cried out in...
Voices drifted out of...
A voice played out of...
A voice rang out down...
A\the voice called out from...
My voice boomed out over...
My voice came out as...
My voice came out in...
My voice came out like...
My voice choked off as...
My voice choked off on...
My voice cracked out like...
My voice cut off as...
My voice dried out as...
My voice dried up in...
My voice drifted off as...
My voice echoed out through...
My voice grated out of...
My voice husked over with...
My voice rang out as...
My voice rose along with...
My voice trailed off as...
My voice trailed off at...
My voice trailed off in...
My voice trailed off into...

My voice trailed off until...
My voice warmed up as...
The voice came out of...
The voice cried out with...
The voice echoed out from...
The voice rose out of...
The voice spoke out of...
The voice trailed off for...

voiced *verb*

I voiced a...
I voiced my...

volunteered *verb*

I volunteered as a...
I volunteered at the...
I volunteered for a\the...
I volunteered from the...
I volunteered in a...

vomit *noun*

Vomit leeched through...
Vomit rose in...
Vomit rushed into...
Vomit spilled out of...
The vomit ran down into...

vomited *verb*

I vomited a\the...
I vomited at a...
I vomited down the...
I vomited in the...
I vomited on the...
I vomited out the...

voted *verb*

I voted against a...
I voted on the...

vowed *verb*

I vowed as a...
I vowed in my...

W

wadded *verb*

I wadded a...
I wadded up the...

waddled *verb*

I waddled across the...
I waddled out an...
I waddled to the...
I waddled up the...
I waddled out into the...
I waddled out of the...
I waddled over to the...

waded *verb*

I waded across the...
I waded along the...
I waded into a\the...
I waded through the...
I waded to the...
I waded down into the...
I waded out of the...
I waded out onto the...

wafted *verb*

I wafted the...

waged *verb*

I waged a...

wagged *verb*

I wagged a...
I wagged my...

waggled *verb*

I waggled a\an\the...

I waggled my...

wagon *noun*

The wagon bore down on...

wailed *verb*

I wailed a\the...
I wailed at the...

waist *noun*

My waist went in...

waited *verb*

I waited a\an\the...
I waited my...
I waited as a\the...
I waited at a\the...
I waited before the...
I waited behind a...
I waited beneath the...
I waited by my...
I waited by the...
I waited for a\an\the...
I waited for my...
I waited in a\the...
I waited in my...
I waited on a\the...
I waited on my...
I waited out the...
I waited through the...
I waited till the...
I waited under a...
I waited until a\an\the...
I waited until my...
I waited while the...
I waited with the...
I waited within the...
I waited around in my...

walked *verb*

I walked a\the...

I walked my...
I walked about the...
I walked across a\the...
I walked against the...
I walked along a\the...
I walked alongside an\the...
I walked among the...
I walked amongst the...
I walked around a\the...
I walked around my...
I walked as a...
I walked at an\the...
I walked behind a\the...
I walked beside the...
I walked between my...
I walked between the...
I walked by a\the...
I walked down a\the...
I walked for a\the...
I walked from my...
I walked from the...
I walked in a\the...
I walked in my...
I walked inside a\the...
I walked into a\an\the...
I walked into my...
I walked like a\an...
I walked off the...
I walked on a\the...
I walked on my...
I walked onto the...
I walked out a\the...
I walked outside the...
I walked over a\the...
I walked past a\an\the...
I walked past my...
I walked through a\an\the...
I walked to a\an\the...
I walked to my...
I walked toward a\an\the...
I walked toward my...
I walked towards a\the...

I walked under a\the...
I walked until the...
I walked up a\the...
I walked up my...
I walked with a\an\the...
I walked with my...
I walked across to the...
I walked along at the...
I walked along outside the...
I walked around so the...
I walked around to my...
I walked around to the...
I walked down into the...
I walked off at a...
I walked off into the...
I walked off to my...
I walked off to the...
I walked off toward a...
I walked off towards the...
I walked off with the...
I walked on to the...
I walked out into the...
I walked out of my...
I walked out of the...
I walked out on the...
I walked out onto the...
I walked out through the...
I walked out to a\the...
I walked out to my...
I walked out under the...
I walked out with a\an\the...
I walked over from the...
I walked over to a\an\the...
I walked over to my...
I walked over with my...
I walked through to my...
I walked through to the...
I walked up to the...

walkway *noun*
A walkway dropped down along...

wall *noun*

Walls soared up around...
The wall lit up as...
The wall materialized out of...
The wall shot out along...

wandered *verb*

I wandered a\an\the...
I wandered about the...
I wandered among the...
I wandered around the...
I wandered beneath the...
I wandered down an\the...
I wandered for a...
I wandered into a\the...
I wandered on the...
I wandered past the...
I wandered through a\the...
I wandered toward the...
I wandered around for a...
I wandered off into the...
I wandered off to the...
I wandered out into the...
I wandered out on my...
I wandered out to the...
I wandered over for a...
I wandered over to a\the...

wanted *verb*

I wanted a\an\the...
I wanted my...
I wanted after a...
I wanted as the...
I wanted in a\the...
I wanted in my...
I wanted on my...
I wanted with a...
I wanted out of the...

wariness *noun*

Wariness rose in...
Wariness swam behind...

warmed *verb*

I warmed my...
I warmed the...
I warmed up the...

warmth *noun*

Warmth bloomed in...
Warmth blossomed in...
Warmth boiled through...
Warmth flashed in...
Warmth flowed through...
Warmth pulsed through...
Warmth seeped into...
Warmth shot through...
Warmth sprayed across...
Warmth stole over...
Warmth swept in...
Warmth traveled through...
A warmth began in
A warmth came with
A warmth surged through
My warmth bled into...
The warmth ran down over...

warned *verb*

I warned my...
I warned the...

warning *noun*

A warning popped up on...

washed *verb*

I washed a\the...
I washed my...
I washed at the...
I washed away the...
I washed down my...
I washed down the...

I washed off my...
I washed off the...
I washed out a...
I washed out my...
I washed off in the...
I washed out on my...
I washed up at the...
I washed up in a...
I washed up on the...

wasted *verb*

I wasted a\the...
I wasted my...

watched *verb*

I watched a\the...
I watched my...
I watched as a\an\the...
I watched as my...
I watched for a...
I watched for my...
I watched from a\the...
I watched from my...
I watched in my...
I watched in the...
I watched on the...
I watched out my...
I watched out the...
I watched over my...
I watched over the...
I watched through a\the...
I watched until the...
I watched with a...
I watched with my...
I watched without a...

water *noun*

Water beaded on...
Water boiled behind...
Water bounced off...
Water churned in...

Water collected in...
Water condensed on...
Water denoted by...
Water dripped from...
Water drizzled against...
Water erupted onto...
Water exploded in...
Water flooded in...
Water flowed through...
Water geysered in...
Water glimmered in...
Water gushed from...
Water gushed through...
Water gushed with...
Water jetted from...
Water lapped around...
Water poured from...
Water poured in...
Water poured into...
Water ran from...
Water ran like...
Water ran through...
Water rolled beneath...
Water rose over...
Water rushed around...
Water rushed in...
Water slid over...
Water slopped onto...
Water slopped over...
Water sloshed in...
Water sloshed onto...
Water sloshed over...
Water sluiced from...
Water sluiced off...
Water spilled over...
Water splashed against...
Water splashed along...
Water splashed on...
Water sprayed from...
Water sprayed into...
Water spurted from...
Water streamed from...

Water surged from...
Water surged into...
Water swirled at...
Water thundered above...
Water trickled in...
Water washed across...
Water washed over...
Water went in...
My water broke during...
The water came on
The water cascaded over
The water exploded as
The water fell from
The water fell in
The water flowed into
The water got into
The water poured in
The water ran along
The water rose around
The water rushed past
The water slid by
The water spilled from
The water splashed in
The water thundered over
Water rushed up into...
Water flowed down from...
Water foamed up from...
Water gushed out onto...
Water lapped up over...
Water ran out between...
Water ran out through...
Water streamed down from...
Water welled up beneath...
The water roared out of...
The water rose up through...

watered *verb*

I watered my...
I watered the...

waterfall *noun*

A waterfall tumbled out of...

wave *noun*
Waves broke over...
Waves crashed against...
Waves crashed on...
Waves erupted from...

waved *verb*
I waved a\an\the...
I waved my...
I waved around the...
I waved aside the...
I waved at a\the...
I waved at my...
I waved away the...
I waved down my...
I waved for my...
I waved for the...
I waved from the...
I waved in the...
I waved off a\the...
I waved off my...
I waved over the...
I waved to my...
I waved to the...
I waved toward the...
I waved up the...
I waved with my...
I waved with the...
I waved out towards the...

wavered *verb*
I wavered a...
I wavered my...
I wavered at the...
I wavered in my...
I wavered like a...

weakened *verb*
I weakened a...

weakness *noun*
Weakness descended on...

weapon *noun*
The weapon flew across
My weapon flew out of...
The weapon bounced up from...
The weapon leapt out of...
The weapon stuck out from...
The weapon went off as...

weariness *noun*
Weariness blew over...
Weariness descended on...
Weariness descended over...
Weariness fell from...
Weariness flooded through...
Weariness settled on...
Weariness stole over...
Weariness washed over...

weathered *verb*
I weathered the...

weaved *verb*
I weaved a...
I weaved my...
I weaved around the...
I weaved between the...
I weaved through a\the...

wed *verb*
I wed a...

wedged *verb*
I wedged a\the...
I wedged my...
I wedged into the...

week *noun*
Weeks went by...

weighed *verb*
I weighed a\the...
I weighed my...
I weighed down the...

weight *noun*
My weight sank into...
My weight came down on...

welcomed *verb*
I welcomed the...

wended *verb*
I wended my...
I wended past a...

went *verb*
I went a\an\the...
I went my...
I went about my...
I went about the...
I went across the...
I went after my...
I went after the...
I went among the...
I went around a\the...
I went around the...
I went as a...
I went at the...
I went behind a\the...
I went below the...
I went beyond the...
I went by the...
I went down a\the...
I went for a\the...
I went for my...
I went from a\the...

I went from my...
I went in a\the...
I went in my...
I went inside the...
I went into a\an\the...
I went into my...
I went off my...
I went off the...
I went on a\an\the...
I went on my...
I went onto the...
I went out a\the...
I went out my...
I went over a\the...
I went over my...
I went past my...
I went past the...
I went though the...
I went through a\the...
I went through my...
I went to a\an\the...
I went to my...
I went toward my...
I went toward the...
I went towards the...
I went under an\the...
I went up the...
I went with a\an\the...
I went with my...
I went without the...
I went around in a...
I went around to my...
I went around to the...
I went down by the...
I went down for the...
I went down from the...
I went down in a...
I went down into the...
I went down like a...
I went down on my...
I went down on the...
I went down onto the...

I went down over the...
I went down through the...
I went down to the...
I went down with a...
I went down with my...
I went off into the...
I went off on the...
I went off to the...
I went on to the...
I went out after a...
I went out for a...
I went out for my...
I went out from the...
I went out in the...
I went out into the...
I went out of my...
I went out of the...
I went out on a\the...
I went out onto the...
I went out through the...
I went out to my...
I went out to the...
I went out with a\the...
I went out with my...
I went over for a...
I went over to a\an\the...
I went over to my...
I went through into the...
I went through on a...
I went through to my...
I went through to the...
I went through with my...
I went up on my...
I went up over the...
I went up to my...
I went up to the...
I went up with my...

wept *verb*

I wept my...
I wept at the...

I wept for a\the...
I wept for my...
I wept in the...
I wept into my...
I wept until the...

wet *verb*

I wet a\the...
I wet my...

whacked *verb*

I whacked the...

wheeled *verb*

I wheeled a\the...
I wheeled my...
I wheeled around the...
I wheeled beneath an...
I wheeled in a...
I wheeled into a...
I wheeled out a\the...
I wheeled toward the...
I wheeled around as the...
I wheeled around at the...
I wheeled around in a\the...
I wheeled around to the...

wheeze *noun*

A wheeze kicked up in...

wheezed *verb*

I wheezed in a...

whimper *noun*

Whimpers tore from...
A whimper came out of...

whimpered *verb*

I whimpered a...
I whimpered like a...

whipped *verb*

I whipped a\an\the...
I whipped my...
I whipped off my...
I whipped out a\the...
I whipped out my...
I whipped up my...
I whipped up the...
I whipped around at the...
I whipped over onto my...

whirled *verb*

I whirled the...
I whirled in my...
I whirled on my...
I whirled through an\the...
I whirled around as the...
I whirled around at the...
I whirled around with the...

whisper *noun*

Whispers circulated among...
Whispers said that...
Whispers sprang up throughout...

whispered *verb*

I whispered a\an\the...
I whispered my...
I whispered in my...
I whispered in the...
I whispered into my...
I whispered into the...
I whispered of a...
I whispered on the...
I whispered through my...
I whispered to my...
I whispered to the...
I whispered under my...
I whispered with the...

whistled *verb*

I whistled a...
I whistled around the...
I whistled as my...
I whistled between my...
I whistled for the...
I whistled into the...
I whistled through my...
I whistled to the...

whizzed *verb*

I whizzed around the...

widened *verb*

I widened my...
I widened the...

wielded *verb*

I wielded a\the...
I wielded my...

wiggled *verb*

I wiggled a\the...
I wiggled my...
I wiggled off the...
I wiggled over the...

willed *verb*

I willed a\the...
I willed my...

wilted *verb*

I wilted in the...
I wilted under my...

winced *verb*

I winced a...
I winced as a\the...
I winced at the...
I winced because the...

I winced from the...
I winced through a...
I winced with a...

wind *noun*

Wind blew across...
Wind blew through...
Wind gusted across...
Wind hissed in...
Wind howled over...
Wind howled through...
Wind moaned in...
Wind moaned though...
Wind moaned through...
Wind represented by...
Wind rushed in...
Wind sliced across...
Wind swirled over...
Wind whipped at...
Wind whispered through...
Wind whistled in...
Wind whistled inside...
Wind whistled past...
A wind came out of...
A wind kicked up off...
A wind picked up that...
The wind came down from...
The wind howled down off...
The wind picked up as...
The wind picked up from...
The wind picked up in...
The wind reached out for...
The wind shrieked out of...

window *noun*

Windows broke like...
Windows opened into...
A window popped up on...
The windows looked out over...

wine *noun*

Wine dribbled from...
Wine sloshed over...
Wine splashed into...

winged *verb*

I winged across the...

winked *verb*

I winked at my...
I winked at the...
I winked over my...

winter *noun*

Winter came with...

wiped *verb*

I wiped a\an\the...
I wiped my...
I wiped at my...
I wiped at the...
I wiped away a\the...
I wiped away my...
I wiped down a\the...
I wiped off my...
I wiped off the...
I wiped up the...
I wiped off about a...

wired *verb*

I wired my...

wisdom *noun*

Wisdom flooded into...

wished *verb*

I wished a\an\the...
I wished my...
I wished for a\the...
I wished for my...

wistfulness *noun*

Wistfulness tugged on...

withdrew *verb*

I withdrew a\the...
I withdrew my...
I withdrew after the...
I withdrew from my...
I withdrew from the...
I withdrew into my...
I withdrew into the...
I withdrew to the...

withheld *verb*

I withheld a...

witnessed *verb*

I witnessed a\the...
I witnessed my...

wobbled *verb*

I wobbled a...
I wobbled my...
I wobbled across the...
I wobbled for a...
I wobbled on my...
I wobbled to my...

woke *verb*

I woke a\the...
I woke my...
I woke as the...
I woke before my...
I woke before the...
I woke from a\an...
I woke from my...
I woke in a\the...
I woke on my...
I woke on the...
I woke to a\the...

I woke to my...
I woke up a\an\the...
I woke with a\the...
I woke with my...
I woke up at a...
I woke up at my...
I woke up before my...
I woke up behind the...
I woke up from a...
I woke up in a\an\the...
I woke up in my...
I woke up on a\the...
I woke up on my...
I woke up to the...
I woke up with a...
I woke up with my...

wolfed *verb*

I wolfed the...
I wolfed down my...
I wolfed down the...

won *verb*

I won a\the...
I won my...
I won by a...
I won in the...
I won like a...

wonder *noun*

Wonder came into...

wondered *verb*

I wondered a\the...
I wondered about my...
I wondered about the...
I wondered after the...
I wondered at my...
I wondered at the...
I wondered for a\the...
I wondered if a\the...

I wondered if my...
I wondered whether the...

word *noun*

Words came in...
Words died in...
Words fell from...
Words rose from...
Words spilled from...
My words broke into...
My words came in...
My words crashed among...
My words disappeared as...
My words drifted because...
My words dropped like...
My words fell into...
My words rang against...
My words rang with...
My words rubbed over...
My words sank in...
My words skipped across...
My words stayed with...
My words went into...
The words appeared in
The words blurred on
The words came from
The words came in
The words came like
The words came through
The words came without
The words died in
The words died on
The words drifted at
The words emerged before
The words fell like
The words felt like
The words flowed from
The words froze in
The words rang in
The words rang through
The words rose like

The words sang in
The words sank into
The words seemed like
The words slammed into
The words slipped from
The words sounded like
The words streamed from
The words swam in
The words tore from
The words tumbled in
The words uttered by
The words wavered as
The words went through
Words backed up in...
Words tumbled out of...
Words welled up in...
My words broke up in...
My words came out in...
My words came out like...
My words carried over in...
My words choked off with...
My words cut off as...
My words died out as...
My words dried up in...
My words drifted off as...
My words slipped off as...
My words trailed off as...
My words trailed off because...
My words trailed off in...
My words trailed off on...
My words tumbled out in...
The word came down from...
The word came out in...
The word came out with...
The word dropped out of...
The word flew out of...
The word slipped out before...
The word stuck out like...
The words banged around in...
The words blurted out of...
The words bounced around
inside...

The words breathed out in...
The words came out as...
The words came out in...
The words came out of...
The words cried out in...
The words dried up in...
The words dried up on...
The words drifted off as...
The words drifted off into...
The words fell out of...
The words floated out of...
The words leaked out of...
The words poured out in...
The words poured out of...
The words ran out of...
The words rasped out of...
The words rolled out across...
The words rolled out in...
The words rushed out of...
The words sawed out of...
The words seized up in...
The words shot out like...
The words slipped out before...
The words spewed out in...
The words spilled out of...
The words tumbled out in...
The words tumbled out of...

wore *verb*

I wore a\an\the...
I wore my...
I wore during my...
I wore on my...
I wore to the...
I wore upon my...

worked *verb*

I worked a\an\the...
I worked my...
I worked around the...
I worked as a\an\the...

I worked at a\the...
I worked for a\an\the...
I worked from a\the...
I worked in a\an\the...
I worked in my...
I worked like a\an...
I worked off my...
I worked on a\the...
I worked on my...
I worked out an\the...
I worked through a\the...
I worked through my...
I worked toward my...
I worked under the...
I worked until the...
I worked up a\the...
I worked with a\the...
I worked out of the...
I worked out with the...

world *noun*

The world broke up into...
The world fell out of...

worried *verb*

I worried the...
I worried about my...
I worried about the...
I worried at the...
I worried for a\the...
I worried for my...
I worried over the...

worry *noun*

Worry bled through...
Worry clutched at...
Worry crowded in...
Worry lanced through...
Worry mingled with...
Worry seeped into...
My worries disappeared into...

The worry went out of...

worshiped *verb*

I worshiped my...

worshipped *verb*

I worshipped the...

wound *noun*

My wound closed while...

wound *verb*

I wound a\the...
I wound my...
I wound along the...
I wound among the...
I wound around the...
I wound between the...
I wound down my...
I wound down the...
I wound through the...
I wound up the...
I wound up with a\the...

wove *verb*

I wove a\the...
I wove my...
I wove through the...

wracked *verb*

I wracked my...

wrapped *verb*

I wrapped a\an\the...
I wrapped my...
I wrapped up my...
I wrapped up the...
I wrapped up about the...

wrath *noun*

My wrath exploded like...

wrecked *verb*
I wrecked an...

wrenched *verb*
I wrenched my...
I wrenched the...
I wrenched at the...
I wrenched off my...
I wrenched open the...

wrestled *verb*
I wrestled the...
I wrestled for a...
I wrestled in the...
I wrestled with a\the...
I wrestled with my...

wriggled *verb*
I wriggled my...
I wriggled the...
I wriggled around a...
I wriggled in my...
I wriggled into the...
I wriggled like a...
I wriggled onto the...
I wriggled toward the...
I wriggled under the...
I wriggled down in the...
I wriggled down into the...
I wriggled down under the...
I wriggled out of my...
I wriggled out of the...

wrinkled *verb*
I wrinkled my...
I wrinkled up my...

wrist *noun*

My wrists felt like...

writhed *verb*
I writhed a...
I writhed against the...
I writhed along the...
I writhed as the...
I writhed at the...
I writhed in the...
I writhed on my...
I writhed on the...
I writhed under the...
I writhed with the...

wrote *verb*
I wrote a\an\the...
I wrote my...
I wrote about a\the...
I wrote about my...
I wrote as a...
I wrote at the...
I wrote down an\the...
I wrote for a\the...
I wrote in a\an\the...
I wrote in my...
I wrote like a...
I wrote of my...
I wrote on a\the...
I wrote out a\the...
I wrote to the...
I wrote until my...
I wrote with an...

wrung *verb*
I wrung my...
I wrung out the...

Y

yanked *verb*

I yanked a\the...
I yanked my...
I yanked at my...
I yanked at the...
I yanked away the...
I yanked down my...
I yanked down the...
I yanked from the...
I yanked off my...
I yanked off the...
I yanked on a\the...
I yanked on my...
I yanked open a\the...
I yanked open my...
I yanked out a\the...
I yanked out my...
I yanked up my...
I yanked down on my...

year *noun*

Years slipped by...
Years went by...
Years went into...

yearned *verb*

I yearned for the...

yelled *verb*

I yelled a\the...
I yelled across the...
I yelled at a\the...
I yelled at my...
I yelled for a\the...
I yelled for my...

I yelled from the...
I yelled in the...
I yelled into a\the...
I yelled over my...
I yelled over the...
I yelled through my...
I yelled to the...
I yelled up the...
I yelled down into the...

yelped *verb*

I yelped in a...
I yelped into the...
I yelped like a...

yielded *verb*

I yielded my...
I yielded to the...
I yielded up my...

Z

zeroed *verb*
I zeroed the...

zigzagged *verb*
I zigzagged between the...
I zigzagged through the...

zipped *verb*
I zipped my...
I zipped the...
I zipped into my...
I zipped through the...
I zipped up my...
I zipped up the...
I zipped off to the...
I zipped over to the...

zoomed *verb*
I zoomed into the...
I zoomed out on the...

www.ingramcontent.com/pod-product-compliance
Lightning Source LLC
Chambersburg PA
CBHW051436250726
48655CB00001B/96